How to Do Everything with YouTube

About the Author

Chad Fahs is an author and digital filmmaker. His work as author and coauthor includes several books on video and filmmaking, as well as on After Effects, Final Cut Pro, DVD Studio Pro, Flash MX, Mac OS X, iPod, and iTunes. In addition, he has written technology reviews for *Wired Magazine* and created course-ware and training materials for a variety of clients. Chad is also an Apple Certified Trainer and teaches classes in editing and DVD authoring for training centers around the country, including Future Media Concepts. As a digital filmmaker, Chad has created videos and animations for a wide array of projects, including documentaries, music videos, electronic press kits, commercials, and experimental films. He has worked as an editor and animator at Concrete Pictures in Philadelphia and continues to create video and multimedia projects. Currently, Chad is finishing work on a documentary and assisting with digital media in the Communication Department at Villanova University. For more information, visit his home page at www.chadfahs.com.

How to Do Everything with YouTube

Chad Fahs

New York   Chicago   San Francisco   Lisbon
London   Madrid   Mexico City   Milan   New Delhi
San Juan   Seoul   Singapore   Sydney   Toronto

The McGraw·Hill Companies

Cataloging-in-Publication Data is on file with the Library of Congress

How to Do Everything with YouTube

1234567890   FGR FGR   01987

ISBN   978-0-07-149865-4
MHID   0-07-149865-6

Sponsoring Editor
Roger Stewart

Editorial Supervisor
Patty Mon

Project Manager
Harleen Chopra,
International Typesetting
and Composition

Acquisitions Coordinator
Carly Stapleton

Technical Editor
Jennifer Ackerman Kettell

Copy Editor
Lisa McCoy

Proofreader
Linda Leggio

Indexer
Broccoli Information
Management

Production Supervisor
Jean Bodeaux

Composition
International Typesetting
and Composition

Illustration
International Typesetting
and Composition

Art Director, Cover
Jeff Weeks

Cover Designer
Pattie Lee

This book is dedicated to my family and friends.

Contents at a Glance

Contents

Acknowledgments

I would like to thank all of those who were involved in the creation of this book, including the editors at McGraw-Hill, Roger Stewart, Carly Stapleton, Jenn Kettell, Lisa McCoy, and Harleen Chopra, as well as my agent Carole McClendon. In addition, I would like to thank those who contributed their thoughts and experiences to the book through interviews, including Brooke Brodack, Damian Kulash, Scott Kirsner, Francis Stokes, Matt Sloan, and Adam Yonda. Last, I would like to thank those whose patience and good humor helped me through the writing process, especially Meghann Matwichuk.

Introduction

In 2005, Chad Hurley, Steve Chen, and Jawed Karim launched what would become the most popular video sharing Web site ever created. In fact, until YouTube came along, there were few easy ways to share video on the Web—at least ways that were easy, free, and enjoyable, particularly for the average user. Apart from an inspired idea and creative coding, the success of YouTube was also made possible by the use of Adobe Flash (at that time Macromedia Flash), a plug-in for Web browsers, which has become the de facto standard for delivering multimedia-rich Web sites. With the efficient and ubiquitous FLV (Flash Video) file format as its standard for encoding movies uploaded by users, YouTube made millions of videos instantly accessible by the majority of people on the Internet. In addition to the technology that enabled it, YouTube enhanced the experience of watching videos with Web 2.0-inspired social networking features, such as comments, groups, home pages for members, subscriptions, and other community-based ideas made popular through Web sites like MySpace, Facebook, and Friendster, to name a few.

As a result of its simplicity and solid feature set (all free of charge), YouTube's subscriber base quickly grew, and brought with it many talented people who were looking for a place to exhibit their creativity. For the first time, anyone could upload a short film they had made, a video diary, or other home movie and share it with the world. The popularity of a particular video and its creator was bolstered by word of mouth, networking features, and rankings on the site, such as the number of views that a video received. No longer was the success of an individual with a good idea limited to those who could secure corporate sponsorship or large marketing budgets. Professional producers caught on shortly thereafter, and YouTube has since become a major stopping point on the marketing circuit, even for traditional media outlets. In fact, with Google's acquisition of YouTube in 2006, monetary considerations and corporate partnerships are sure to increase. However, YouTube still retains much of its democratic appeal, since the majority of its content is gleefully low-budget, high-creativity material created by average citizens. Ironically, it's this same aesthetic and do-it-yourself ethos that professional outlets have been trying to emulate, often with mixed results.

Since YouTube's launch in 2005, hundreds of millions of users from around the world have used the site, watching videos that other people have posted or uploading videos of their own. The site's popularity has expanded in ways that few could have anticipated (witness the 2008 presidential debates), and its community of users continues to grow and develop new genres of video making. As mentioned, even seasoned video professionals have jumped on board and made use of the cost savings and promotional possibilities of the site to host their product trailers, demos, and other content. However, despite its possibilities as a marketing tool, YouTube's primary purpose is as a place for anyone (regardless of skill level) to upload and share their recorded experiences with other people. Hopefully, within the pages of this book, you will find something to improve your experience of this ever-evolving Web site, and even learn a few things about Web video in general.

What This Book Covers

This book addresses the interests and needs of the casual YouTube user as well as the serious Web enthusiast who is looking to explore YouTube in greater depth. The book begins by exploring the layout of the YouTube Web site and then progresses systematically through many of the features that allow users to create their own videos and upload them to the site. Included in this discussion is an introduction to creating and editing videos for YouTube. More experienced users may find the discussion of YouTube as a promotional tool of interest, sharing in the experience of popular YouTube creators, as discussed in the last chapter.

Chapter 1

Getting Started with YouTube

How to...

- Navigate the YouTube Web site
- Identify important elements of the YouTube interface
- Find videos that you want to watch
- Play a video
- Create a QuickList
- Check viewing history
- Create a new user account

Quick Tour of the YouTube Web Site

Upon arrival at the YouTube Web site, you are greeted by the YouTube home page (see Figure 1-1). The home page is the primary gateway into the world of YouTube, and it

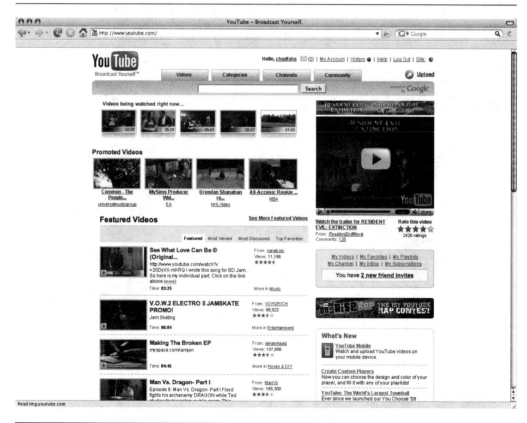

FIGURE 1-1   The YouTube home page

includes a list of Videos being watched right now, Promoted Videos, and Featured Videos, along with a selection of additional links, navigational elements, and a few, relatively, innocuous advertisements.

The list of videos being watched right now is a rotating selection of videos that are (as the title implies) currently being viewed by other YouTube users. This feature is only applicable to users that have the Active Sharing feature turned on for their account, which is discussed in Chapter 5.

The list of promoted videos contains videos that have (seemingly) been chosen on the basis of their popularity, recent number of views, or media partnerships with YouTube. This section of the page is fairly exclusive, and the methods that are used to choose videos may change, particularly when YouTube and its clients want to increase the visibility of a particular video or YouTube user.

The list of featured videos contains those selected by YouTube employees or by a guest editor. If you scroll down the page, you may notice other categories of clips and links listed on the right column, such as What's New, Popular Videos For Mobile Devices, and more. This, of course, represents the current iteration of the YouTube Web site, which will change over time. However, the same basic idea is likely to remain intact—provide quick links on the home page to featured content and other items that YouTube and its parent company Google want to promote (including advertisements and new site features). In fact, it's not a bad idea to start over at the home page every now and again, even if you're comfortable jumping to your own channel (discussed later in this chapter) or to another user's video page directly. If for no other reason, the home page is a good place to get a feel for what YouTube is all about, check out current contests (usually in partnership with an advertiser), and take note of new enhancements to the site.

NOTE
If you'd like to become a guest editor for YouTube and have your favorite videos appear on the home page, send an e-mail to editor@youtube.com with a sample of the videos that you would like to feature.

Along the top of the page are four large tabs for navigating the YouTube Web site. These tabs are part of YouTube's persistent navigation, since no matter which page you are viewing on the site, you have immediate access to the same set of links. In order, from left to right, these tabs are labeled Videos, Categories, Channels, Community. On the far right is an Upload Videos link. Try clicking each tab to view these main areas of the YouTube Web site.

Videos

The Videos tab presents you with a list of 20 videos per page, which you can sort by Most Viewed (the default), Most Recent, Top Rated, Most Discussed, Top Favorites, Most Linked, Recently Featured, Most Responded, and Watch On Mobile (see Figure 1-2). In addition, you can view, or sort, these clips based on units of time, such as Today, This Week, This Month, and All Time. Videos can be sorted by category, too, in case you have a specific type of video in mind, such as music videos that were most viewed this month. You can narrow down your searches

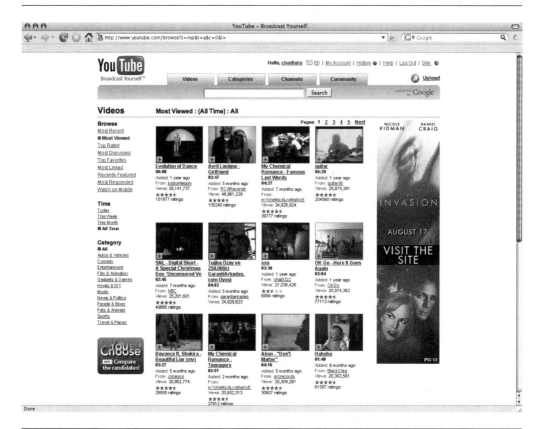

FIGURE 1-2 You can browse videos according to many different criteria using the Videos tab.

by typing keywords into the Search box in the upper-right corner of the Web site. Searching for videos is discussed later in this chapter.

NOTE *When you click a specific set of criteria, such as Most Viewed (listed on the left side of the page), a little red dot appears next to the currently selected option.*

Categories

If you prefer to browse for videos according to a specific area of interest, such as Comedy, Film & Animation, News & Politics, and Pets & Animals (to name a few), you can start with the Categories tab (see Figure 1-3). On the left side of the page are all of the categories you can choose from.

FIGURE 1-3   The Categories tab sorts videos according to the kind of content they contain.

When All is the selected category, you are presented with a Pick of The Day, which is a specially selected video that is embedded at the top of the page, along with a few Featured Channels. Underneath, you will see the individual categories listed again (Featured Videos By Category), each with its own thumbnail that represents the featured video (Editor's Pick) for that category. Each category that you select has its own main page with its own favorite pick (on individual category pages, the featured video is referred to as the Editor's Pick), an embedded video, and a selection of additional featured videos and channels. This is akin to the YouTube home page, except the content is targeted to the specific category you've selected. As with the Videos tab, once you've narrowed down your search criteria by category, you can further refine the results by entering keywords into the Search box.

The following is a list of YouTube categories and the descriptions provided by YouTube for each of them:

- **Autos & Vehicles**   Cars, racing, accessorizing, and more
- **Comedy**   Sketches, standup, spoofs, and more
- **Entertainment**   Movies and television
- **Film & Animation**   Short films, stop-motion, animation, and more
- **Gadgets & Games**   Products, video games, technology, and more
- **How to & DIY**   Instruction, training, and more
- **Music**   Bands, singers, songwriters, and more
- **News & Politics**   Current events and commentaries
- **People & Blogs**   Personalities, biographies, artists, and more
- **Pets & Animals**   Dogs, cats, hamsters, and more
- **Sports**   Extreme, competitions, skateboarding, and more
- **Travel & Places**   Vacations, nature, monuments, and more

Channels

Visitors to YouTube can view the contents of a member's channel in order to access all of the videos that this person has uploaded (see Figure 1-4). Channels are particularly useful for viewing a series of videos uploaded by the same member, such as all of the videos posted by the creators of Ask A Ninja, whose channel name is actually listed as digitalfilmmaker. In fact, every member of YouTube has their own channel where they can upload videos, post personal information in their profile (similar to www.MySpace.com), and engage in a variety of other activities that draw users to their personal page (which is discussed in Chapter 5). In other words, each channel is the personal home page of an official YouTube member, containing all of their videos and other profile information. Becoming a member of YouTube requires setting up an account (covered later in this chapter), after which you are able to upload videos and customize your channel. You can also subscribe to another member's channel, and other members can subscribe to yours.

The Channels tab can be navigated by selecting from different channel types, including Comedians, Directors, Gurus, Musicians, Partners, Sponsors, and certain special types, such as the current (as of this writing) channel type for the 2008 U.S. presidential elections, YouChoose08. In addition, you can sort channels according to most subscribed (this is the default) and most viewed; browsing criteria; or by units of time, including this week, this month, or all time.

Community

The Community tab consists of ways that members can engage in collective activities, such as viewing and joining groups, participating in contests, and more (see Figure 1-5). Detailed coverage of features related to the Community tab is found in Chapter 5.

FIGURE 1-4 The Channels tab is useful if you want to view videos by a specific type of YouTube member (such as a musician).

Upload

If you have set up an account with YouTube, you can upload your own videos to the site for other people to view (see Figure 1-6). This can be done using videos you've captured and stored on your computer's hard drive or by uploading directly from a webcam or mobile phone. Uploading videos is further discussed in Chapter 4.

Localized (International) Sites

YouTube has created localized versions of its site for different countries in order to feature content and languages that are most pertinent to global users. You can access these alternate versions of the site by clicking the Site link or the globe-and-flag icon in the upper-right corner

The Community tab provides easy access to Groups, Contests, and other social features of the YouTube Web site.

of the YouTube Web site (see Figure 1-7). Currently, there are nine countries listed—Brazil, France, Ireland, Italy, Japan, Netherlands, Poland, Spain, and United Kingdom, in addition to the Global (United States) site. All of the same YouTube content is available to users, regardless of the country they have chosen as their preference. However, the featured content, as well as the language that appears (especially notable on the home page), will change based on the country that is chosen.

TestTube

On occasion, YouTube adds special beta (in testing) features to the site, which are primarily accessible through the TestTube page (see Figure 1-8). YouTube refers to TestTube as its ideas "incubator." It's where you can try out features that are (perhaps) not fully functional or that still

FIGURE 1-6   Once you've set up an account with YouTube, you can visit the Upload tab to submit your videos to the site.

FIGURE 1-7   YouTube offers localized content for a variety of countries and languages.

FIGURE 1-8 You can preview the latest YouTube innovations by visiting the TestTube page.

require feedback from users. You can access the TestTube page by clicking the TestTube link at the bottom of most YouTube pages (located under the section labeled YouTube, along with several other site-related links) or by going directly to http://youtube.com/testtube. You will learn about special TestTube features as you work through this book, such as Active Sharing, AudioSwap, Remixer, and Streams.

Blog

Another special page that you may find of interest is the official YouTube blog, which is maintained by employees of YouTube and features information about new features, site updates, contests, and other news related to the operation of the Web site (see Figure 1-9). You can access the YouTube blog by clicking the Blog link at the bottom of any YouTube page (located under the section labeled YouTube, along with several other site-related links) or by going directly to http://youtube.com/blog.

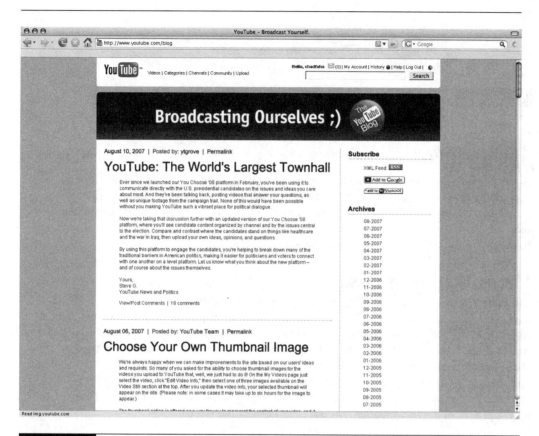

FIGURE 1-9   Stay up to date on current YouTube news and site features by visiting the official YouTube blog.

Searching for Videos

When you have an idea of what you want to watch, oftentimes, the easiest way to find it is by using the Search box, located in the middle of the top and bottom areas of most YouTube pages (see Figure 1-10). Simply type the keywords you want to search by, and click the Search button, just as you would use a search engine like Google. It appears that YouTube's search capabilities are currently limited to simple queries, lacking true Boolean search operations (specifically OR, NOT, and parentheses to nest search items). Given the other ways that you can narrow your searches with the browsing criteria in the Video and Category tabs, basic searches on multiple keywords is often adequate. By using quotations, you can also search for exact phrases.

Playing a Video

Now that you've been oriented to the general layout of the YouTube Web site, it's time to explore the reason that we are here: to watch videos. After all, this is the primary reason why people come to the site. Only after getting turned on to the types of videos you can create do most people make the leap and upload videos of their own. To begin, let's take a look at the basic ways videos are presented for our viewing enjoyment.

Videos That You Browse

Browsing videos is simple with YouTube. Whether you're accessing YouTube through the home page, the Videos tab, or even from within the page of a currently playing video, you will almost certainly see lists of videos that you can jump to. Often, these are videos that YouTube considers similar to the content you are currently viewing (based on associated keywords and tags), while other times they are hand-picked for the YouTube community (see Featured Videos, for example, on the home page), or they are sorted according to a list of specific criteria (see Figure 1-11). In any case, videos are presented for browsing and selecting in a few basic ways, even though they may appear in slightly different layouts, sizes, or areas of the screen.

Thumbnails

Thumbnails are a single frame pulled from the videos that a member submits to YouTube. They represent the contents of a video and act as visual clues when browsing, but are not always accurate depictions of what a video is about. When you upload your own videos, thumbnails are created by automatically selecting a frame from the middle point of your video.

Titles

Every video needs a title, which acts as a personal identifier, just as the title of a movie or book needs something to identify it. On YouTube, the title of a video is usually indicative of its content, but it is not always easy to decipher. Like truncated haikus, many YouTube titles are often quite literal (e.g. "kitten falling asleep") or incredibly nonspecific if you don't know the context (such as "NYC movie premier" or "lazy Sunday"). However, when taken together with a thumbnail and a description, it's not too difficult to figure out the subject.

AMERICA
Favorite American Pastimes Public Domain Footage
(Courtesy of Prelinger Archives) Created by **Chad**
Fahs - www.chadfahs.com ...Television Religion
Sports Politics War Censorship (more)
Time: **03:09**

★★★★☆
From: chadfahs
Views: 402
Added: 8 months ago

More in Film & Animation

CITY AD
||| Motion ||| Video Art ||| Created by **Chad Fahs**
(www.chadfahs.com) at Concrete Pictures for
MOOV, LAB (more)
Time: **01:36**

★★★★☆
From: chadfahs
Views: 371
Added: 7 months ago

More in Film & Animation

GLOBAL
||| Motion ||| Video Art ||| Created by **Chad Fahs**
(www.chadfahs.com) at Concrete Pictures for
MOOV, LAB (more)
Time: **02:46**

★★★★☆
From: chadfahs
Views: 338
Added: 7 months ago

More in Film & Animation

1-UP
||| Motion ||| Video Art ||| Created by **Chad Fahs**
(www.chadfahs.com) at Concrete Pictures for
MOOV, LAB (more)
Time: **02:29**

★★★★★
From: chadfahs
Views: 307
Added: 7 months ago

More in Film & Animation

1905 REMIX
||| Motion ||| Video Art ||| Created by **Chad Fahs**
(www.chadfahs.com) at Concrete Pictures for
MOOV, LAB (more)
Time: **04:14**

★★★★★
From: chadfahs
Views: 296
Added: 7 months ago

More in Film & Animation

SURVEYOR
||| Motion ||| Video Art ||| Created by **Chad Fahs**
(www.chadfahs.com) at Concrete Pictures for
MOOV, LAB (more)
Time: **03:14**

★★★★★
From: chadfahs
Views: 280
Added: 7 months ago

More in Film & Animation

FIGURE 1-11 YouTube provides basic information about each video that is useful for browsing, although it may be formatted in a variety of ways.

Total Running Time

Underneath each video thumbnail is the total length of the piece, listed in minutes and seconds. This can be an important indicator for a viewer who may not want to watch a 10-minute movie, but is more likely to watch a 30-second clip (or vice versa).

Descriptions

When a member uploads a video, he or she is asked to provide some information about it, including a brief description of its contents. Depending on the industriousness of the member, this description can be several sentences long, but is often just a few words. Ideally, you can use these descriptions to better evaluate the relevance of a particular video when you are browsing or to provide insight on a video you're already viewing, such as where it was shot, who is featured in it, links to relevant Web sites, and so on.

User Names

User names usually appear underneath or to the side of the thumbnail and title for a listed video. Occasionally, they are identified by From or Provided By labels. Clicking a user's name takes you to that particular user's channel, which is their personal video home page. In fact, the user name is also the name of the member's channel, and these terms (user, member, channel) can often be used interchangeably.

Tags

Tags are special keywords and descriptors that are used to identify the videos that you upload to the YouTube site. They provide a form of metadata (essentially, data about data), which is interpreted by YouTube to better sort videos and return relevant search results, even targeted content, based on other videos that you are currently viewing. So, for example, if you are watching a movie trailer for *Spider-Man 3*, then YouTube will find other videos that are tagged similarly (Spider-Man, trailer, movie, etc.) and present them as videos that you can browse alongside the currently playing video. Tags are further discussed in Chapter 4 and Chapter 6.

Date Added

Just as it sounds, this item indicates when the video was uploaded to YouTube. This is another important criterion for sorting videos when you want to browse or refine a search according to date (today, this week, or this month, for example).

Views

YouTube keeps close track of every time a video receives a unique view. The most popular videos are viewed thousands of times and, occasionally, millions of times. By looking at the number of views for a video, you have a gauge of its popularity. More information about views is provided in Chapter 7.

Ratings

When viewers watch a video on YouTube, they have the ability to add a star rating to it in half-star increments, with a five-star maximum rating. The top-rated videos are ranked accordingly on YouTube and are easy to find by going to the Videos tab and clicking Top Rated under the Browse criteria. Rating videos is discussed further in Chapter 5.

Videos That You Play

Once you've located a video that you want to view, click its thumbnail to open its page, with a video embedded for viewing. Notice that there are all of the elements mentioned earlier for videos that you browse, such as title, user name, descriptions, and more. The primary difference here is the layout of the page and the presence of the embedded video player, which automatically starts to load and play back the requested video. Depending on the length of the video and the speed of your Internet connection, it can take a moment or two for playback to begin.

NOTE *The length of a video clip on YouTube is also an indicator of its file size. The FLV video file that resides on YouTube's servers must be loaded into your browser, and clips that are several minutes long may take additional time to preload before reliable playback can be established. If you have a fast Internet connection, then this should not be a real problem. However, even over a fast connection, the YouTube Web site does experience sluggish performance on occasion, due to the number of concurrent users online and a variety of other technical factors. Overall, the experience is surprisingly good, and improvements to expand bandwidth, video quality, and operability are happening all the time.*

The following section describes the features of YouTube's video player and how to use them properly.

Using the YouTube Video Player

The following items are the most utilized controls and panels provided by the YouTube video player, along with a brief description of what each component does (see Figure 1-12):

- ■ **Viewer window** This window is the screen where your video plays back, usually at the default size specified by YouTube, or sometimes at a custom size if the player is embedded in a Web page.

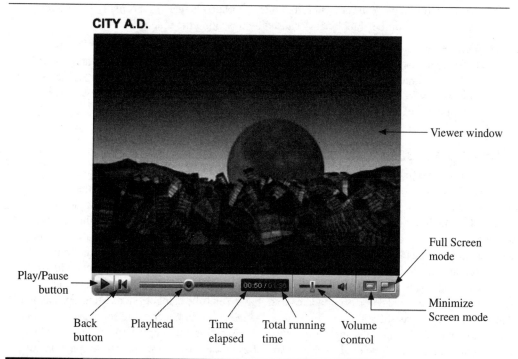

FIGURE 1-12   The YouTube video player is used to watch all of YouTube's videos, regardless of where they appear.

- **Play/Pause button**   This button initiates playback and pauses playback when you click it a second time.

- **Back button**   Use this button to return to the beginning of the video clip.

- **Playhead**   Whenever a video is playing in the video player, a playhead indicates the progress of the video and your current location in it. For the portions of the video that have already loaded (indicated by a red progress bar that fills up), you can drag the playhead back and forth to find another point that you want to view in the video without needing to play it at normal speed.

- **Time elapsed/Current time**   Timecode counter (minutes and seconds only) that indicates how much time has elapsed thus far and where you are located within the video clip.

- **Total running time**   This particular clock shows how long the current video clip is from beginning to end.

- **Volume control**   Use the volume controls to increase or decrease the sound levels of your video relative to the sound levels set on your computer.

- **Minimize Screen mode**   Use this mode to shrink your video to its native image resolution when you imported it (usually around 320×240 pixels), rather than having it stretched out to the YouTube-preferred 425×350 pixels that you normally see, thereby reducing some of the "blockiness" caused by upscaling the video.

- **Full Screen mode**   Use this mode to playback the video at full-screen size, scaling it up to fit whatever screen dimensions you are currently using. This mode replicates a real TV feel by eliminating the browser and computer desktop altogether. Simply press the ESC key on your keyboard or click the Close button in the lower-right corner of your screen to exit the Full Screen mode.

Watching Videos on iPhone and AppleTV

Apple is among the first companies to adopt support for YouTube through its portable and set-top devices. For example, you can browse and view YouTube content on an iPhone (the revolutionary portable phone, iPod, and Web browser combination introduced by Apple in 2007), which includes a YouTube button on the main user interface. At the time of this writing, only the most popular content and new additions are available through this device, although the entire catalog of YouTube videos should be available shortly (once they are converted to the H.264 format). In addition, AppleTV includes the ability to browse and view YouTube videos, just as you would view your other iTunes content (both AppleTV and the iPhone use iTunes software to sync media and perform updates), adding a YouTube category to existing options like Movies, Music, Podcasts, Photos, and more (see Figure 1-13). In general, the same principles for navigating and identifying YouTube content through a Web browser applies to YouTube content that is viewed on one of these devices. For more information, visit www.apple.com/iphone and www.apple.com/appletv.

FIGURE 1-13   AppleTV allows you to browse and watch YouTube videos on your television.

TIP   *If your AppleTV is not currently set up to view YouTube videos, navigate to your AppleTV Settings menu and choose Update Software.*

Creating a QuickList

When you find a video that you'd like to save for later viewing, or if you simply prefer to collect a list of videos and watch them all at one time (like using a shopping cart system), you may want to check out QuickLists. A QuickList is a temporary list of videos you can add to while browsing the YouTube Web site. This list is temporarily stored in your browser's memory and disappears when you exit your browser or shut down your computer. The following steps demonstrate how to create and view a QuickList.

1. Locate a video you want to watch by using the Search box in the upper-right corner of any YouTube Web page or by browsing through the Video and Category tabs.

2. Once you've located a video you want to watch, click the plus sign (+) symbol in the lower-left corner of the video's thumbnail to add it to your QuickList (see Figure 1-14).

NOTE   *In order to see the plus sign on a video thumbnail, you need to be looking at videos on a browseable page (or similar mode), not on the page where a video plays.*

3. Repeat steps 1 and 2 a few more times, continuing to browse for videos until you've collected several more items for your QuickList.

FIGURE 1-14   Click the plus sign on a thumbnail to add it to your QuickList.

4. Click a video's thumbnail to open its video page. Notice that underneath the video player is a gray bar titled QuickList with a Play All button, a Play Next button, and an arrow that opens a window to access individual clips (see Figure 1-15). If you are using the new beta page, these items will appear on the right side of the screen under a section labeled Unsaved Playlist.

NOTE   *The QuickList bar under the video player does not display until you've added items to create a QuickList.*

5. If it's not already open, click the special QuickList button (the downward-pointing arrow) underneath the video player on the right to open the hidden window with all of your QuickList items inside (see Figure 1-16).

6. Click the Show All Videos button at the bottom of the QuickList window, and then click one of the videos in the QuickList to watch it. If you are using the new beta page, you can click a video from the Unsaved Playlist area to watch it.

7. Delete one of the QuickList items by clicking its trashcan icon on the far-right side of the list. Notice that the running time for each video is listed on the right as well.

8. If you don't care to save individual QuickList items, select the Remove Videos As I Watch Them check box on the lower-left corner of the QuickList window.

9. Click the Play All button at the bottom of the video player (at the top of the QuickList) to watch all of the remaining videos. If you are using the new beta page, you can click Play All next to Unsaved Playlist.

FIGURE 1-15   When you've added items to a QuickList, the relevant options appear beneath every video player on YouTube (with the exception of the new beta page).

FIGURE 1-16   The QuickList window contains all of the clips you added to the QuickList.

> NOTE
>
> *QuickLists are different from playlists. A QuickList is temporary, limited in its functionality, and you do not need an account to create one. Playlists are "permanent" lists of videos that you can create and store if you have a member account. You can learn more about playlists, including how to share them, in Chapter 5.*

Checking Your Viewing History

YouTube includes a convenient feature that allows you to find videos you've recently watched (see Figure 1-17). It does this by accessing session information from your browser. At this point, some readers may wonder if YouTube stores this information and tracks their activities on the Web site. According to YouTube's current privacy policy, they may store some of the information that you provide to the site, including links that you click (which may include videos that you've watched). If you are concerned about issues of privacy, make sure that you refer to YouTube's latest privacy notice at http://youtube.com/t/privacy for more information.

You can view your history by simply clicking the History link at the top of most YouTube Web pages. The Viewing History tab is displayed, and you can look through and access any of the recently watched videos. In addition, you can clear your history by clicking the Clear Viewing History link in the lower-right corner of the Viewing History tab.

Setting Up a Basic YouTube Account

As you learned in the introduction, YouTube provides a free service to everyone. This is, in large part, the secret of YouTube's success: provide videos that everyone can view and accounts for anyone who wants to upload their own content. In this way, the site builds itself, using content generated by users like you. Although you do not need to register in order to watch videos,

The Viewing History tab shows your recently watched videos.

you do need to create a logon identity and user name to upload your own videos. In addition to uploading videos, only registered users can take full advantage of the special features that YouTube has to offer, like creating playlists, posting comments, joining a stream, or establishing a vlog (video Web log). These features, and many others, are awaiting you inside YouTube, once you complete the simple sign-up process (see Figure 1-18).

The following steps demonstrate how to set up a new account and become an official member of YouTube.

1. Click the Sign Up button in the upper-right corner of the YouTube Web page.

2. From the Account Type pop-up window, select Standard, Director, Musician, Comedian, or Guru. Initially, you can choose Standard, since it's easy to change the account type later. YouTube allows you to specify the type of account you want to create, while giving you the ability to easily switch it at a later time. Each account type has its own benefits, depending on the specific type of user or content creator, which includes (most notably) having your

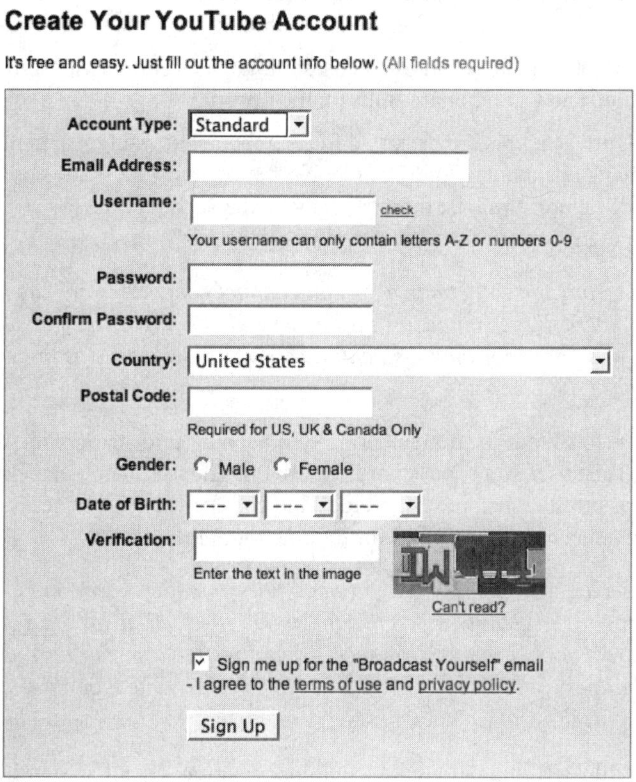

Create Your YouTube Account

It's free and easy. Just fill out the account info below. (All fields required)

Account Type: Standard ▾

Email Address:

Username: check
Your username can only contain letters A-Z or numbers 0-9

Password:

Confirm Password:

Country: United States ▾

Postal Code:
Required for US, UK & Canada Only

Gender: ○ Male   ○ Female

Date of Birth: --- ▾ --- ▾ --- ▾

Verification:
Enter the text in the image
Can't read?

☑ Sign me up for the "Broadcast Yourself" email
- I agree to the terms of use and privacy policy.

Sign Up

FIGURE 1-18   It's fast and easy to sign up for a new YouTube account.

account listed alongside other users with the same account type. Customization options vary according to the type of account that you create, so choosing the best account type will help you to manage your videos better. Fortunately, you do not need to decide right now which type of account is best for you. Later, after you have some videos to upload, you can edit your account information and modify the account, or channel type.

■ **Standard User ("YouTuber")**   A standard user (also referred to as a "YouTuber") is the most common account type for YouTube members. Standard accounts have all of the basic features that you need to use YouTube, without the unnecessary, specialized options for customizing your profile.

■ **Director**   Directors are able to use custom items and logos on their profile pages. This type of account is particularly relevant for independent video and filmmakers who want to identify themselves as professional or semiprofessional content creators.

- **Musician**   Musicians are able to use a custom logo, as well as add genre and tour date information to their profiles, along with links to purchase their CDs online.
- **Comedian**   Comedians can use a custom logo, as well as style, show date information, and CD purchase links on their profile.
- **Guru**   Guru accounts are designed for members that want to share their expertise in a particular subject area. For example, if most of your videos are computer tutorials or cooking demonstrations, then this may be the account type for you. Gurus can use a custom logo, genre information, and links to other Web sites.

NOTE *On occasion, YouTube will create a special channel type that is only accessible to selected members. For example, a YouChoose08 channel type (also displayed as Politician), was added for the presidential candidates who are posting videos through the You Choose '08 campaign.*

3. Next, continue to fill out the remainder of your account information, including e-mail address, YouTube user name, password, and so on. The user name that you select will appear in your profile when posting videos and comments, so consider it carefully. Also, be sure to remember your password for logging on to the account.

TIP *Most users tend toward nonsensical, even cryptic-sounding, user names, which help to obscure their true identity, much like the names used online for instant messaging, bulletin boards, or chat rooms. However, if you intend to use your account for more "official" business purposes, it makes sense to select a name that reflects the true identity of yourself, your product, or the company that you represent. The choice is yours.*

4. When you are done filling out your account information, click the Sign Up button.

You're now ready to start using your YouTube account! Don't worry about filling in details for your profile just yet. In the next couple of chapters, you will learn how to create your own videos before uploading them to the YouTube Web site. After you've created some content to add to your channel, you'll learn how to customize it in many different ways.

TIP *If you share a computer, or if you are working on a public computer in a library or office setting, make sure to sign out after each YouTube session. YouTube does not automatically sign off a user, even if you close your browser or restart the computer.*

Chapter 2

Shooting Your Videos

How to...

- Choose what type of video to create
- Select a camcorder
- Operate a video camera
- Create effective compositions
- Make careful lighting choices
- Capture good audio

Now that you've had a tour of YouTube, created an account, and started to watch videos, it's time to create some material of your own. In the next two chapters we discuss how to create videos for YouTube, beginning with the choice of video style and the basic usage of a camera.

Deciding What Kind of Video to Create

The first step to creating a video is deciding what kind of video you want to create. A good place to start is by asking yourself, "What kinds of videos do I like?" If you haven't already decided what type of video you're going to make, take a look at some of the options listed in this section. While we don't cover all possible options (after all, the possibilities are only limited by your creativity), several of the most popular types of videos being created for YouTube are discussed. You'll notice that general categories, such as short films and documentaries, are not covered, since the categorizations on sites like YouTube have become even more specific and difficult to define in traditional terms. New formats are being invented all the time. Perhaps you'll come up with one of your own?

Video Blog (Vlog) and Video Diaries

Video blogs (or "vlog," for short) have come to embody what sites like YouTube are all about—a place where people from all parts of the world can share in the intimate details of each other's life. More accurately, they might be called video diaries, since they are often preoccupied with the minutiae of their subject's day-to-day life (see Figure 2-1). It was a logical step: Since blogs (of the written and pictorial variety) have become so commonplace, why not add video to the mix? Whether it's a serious breakdown of topical news items, a comedic dance routine in front of a webcam, or a "private" confessional, this type of video is well suited to the improvisational and intimate format that YouTube has cultivated since its birth. It's the same sort of format that led to the popularity of YouTube personalities like "lonelygirl15"—whose series of video blogs follow the (fictional) life of a teenage girl named Bree and her friends. While a cleverly constructed phenomenon like "lonelygirl15" was scripted (and begun as a kind of "hoax"), there is really no need for fancy equipment, sets, actors, or even a script. All you need is a video camera or webcam in your home. It's also why the QuickCapture feature was developed for YouTube. Starring in a video blog is a great way to get subscribers, since viewers will (hopefully) want to check back frequently for updates on your life, your loves, or perhaps your unpredictable and infectious sense of humor.

FIGURE 2-1   A video blog can be a personal video diary, an informational report, or other regular video entries posted by a user. (such as brook brodrack).

Video Mashup

According to Wikipedia, a video mashup is "a video that is edited from more than one source to appear as one." Mashups can take many forms, but in most instances are played for comedic effect. For example, movie trailer spoofs are created by re-editing scenes from a film, adding a new soundtrack or voice-over, or combining it with scenes from other movies to make an entirely different story out of the original components. One voice-maker created a trailer for Stanley Kubrick's *The Shining* that recast the movie as a feel-good family drama. Other mashups, like "Ten Things I Hate About Commandments," also recycle old films for comedic effect (see Figure 2-2). During the initial buildup to the 2008 U.S. presidential campaign, admirers of Democratic candidates Barack Obama and Hillary Clinton made a mashup of Apple's iconic Super Bowl ad from 1984 (which was itself referencing a book) called *Vote Different*. While copyright restrictions make mashups legally questionable, they do provide a good way to score a viral video hit. Just don't get sued in the process.

Pets and Animals

Whether we admit it or not, we've all watched them. Videos of cute or silly animals continue to draw a lot of viewers on YouTube. After all, many of the best moments on YouTube are unscripted, and animals are the experts of improvisational comedy (see Figure 2-3). "America's Funniest Home Videos" may have exploited the pet video first (*ad nauseum*), yet there is definitely no shortage of everyday pets and bizarre zoo creatures on the Web, either. So if you've got footage of a talking parakeet or a cat taking a pratfall, why not share it with the world?

FIGURE 2-2 Video mashups create something new out of another work, such as re-editing a film for comedic effect.

FIGURE 2-3 Animal videos are a perennial favorite on YouTube.

Web Series

The video series that are created for YouTube vary widely in subject matter, but they have one thing in common: humor. The concise, serialized nature and sense of comic timing that a good Web series can create makes them an excellent candidate for generating views on YouTube. Perhaps it's the "tune in next week" appeal of a serialized video that hooks viewers or maybe it's just the bite-sized portions of comedy when all you want is a few laughs between breaks at the office or while surfing the Web. Unlike working within a traditional television model, a series created for YouTube can be experimental without risking a big budget or advertiser money. Your series could be a sitcom or a variety show, a spoof on other television programs, or an animated cartoon. In terms of format, a YouTube series like "Ask a Ninja" is very different from "God, Inc.," for example (see Figure 2-4). Still, both are relatively short (each episode is only a few minutes in length) and use humor to draw viewers—simple but important concepts for quickly achieving popularity online.

How-to and Instructional Videos

If you're interested in learning about a particular topic, especially if it's one that involves any sort of visual element to it, then it's likely you'll find someone on YouTube has posted a video about it. Whether it's a demonstration of how to change the oil in your car, an "educational" video on the effects of adding Mentos to Diet Coke, or a video that shows you how to play guitar

FIGURE 2-4   Web series, like God, Inc. (shown here), might incorporate elements of traditional video series (in this case, a show like *The Office*) in a much more compact form.

FIGURE 2-5   YouTube can be entertaining and educational.

(see Figure 2-5), YouTube users are creating them. In fact, YouTube has created an account type called "Guru" for just the sort of people who like to create these videos. The sharing of knowledge that's possible with instructional videos on YouTube has great potential. If you're an expert in any area, or if you simply have a hobby or particular skill that you'd like to share with others, you can shoot a video about it and upload it to YouTube.

Music Videos

Music videos are fairly self-explanatory, since most of us are familiar with them from sources like MTV (when they were still playing music) or from DVDs by our favorite artists. However, why not create a music video that is uniquely designed for an online viewing experience? You can find many of the same videos you watched in the '80s and '90s available through services like Apple's iTunes, but why not create a video designed for the small screen, which will appeal to more viewers and generate hits for your band? OK Go's "Here It Goes Again" had amazing success and became one of the most watched videos of all time (see Chapter 7 for an interview with the band). They used a simple yet humorous concept, involving treadmills, that was shot with a static camera, and it hit just the right note with viewers (see Figure 2-6).

Political Campaigns

Another offshoot of the video blog or video diary is the political video that speaks directly to the voters. In the recent 2008 presidential campaigns, politicians found that YouTube was a good outreach tool for talking one-on-one with constituents (see Figure 2-7). CNN even jumped on the

FIGURE 2-6   OK Go produced a successful music video for YouTube that used economy, style, and humor.

FIGURE 2-7   YouTube users are encouraged to participate in political discussions with candidates.

bandwagon, teaming up with YouTube for a unique series of debates using questions submitted by YouTube users. If you're running for local office or even for president of the United States, perhaps YouTube is a tool that you can use to get the vote out? However, as with any other public appearance, consider the type of image you want to project, and choose your words and subject matter carefully. There is nothing worse for a political career (or an entertainment career, for that matter) than an embarrassing quote taken out of context in a public forum like YouTube.

Choosing the Right Camera

Whatever type of video you decide to create, it's important to choose the right camera for the job. The camera that you select can have a dramatic effect on how you record your videos and is an important factor in determining the quality of your end results. In addition, make sure that you have the necessary accessories to get the shots you need.

First, you should decide what type of videos you will be recording, as was briefly discussed in the last section. For example, if you are only recording video diaries, then a webcam may suffice (see Figure 2-8). If you intend to shoot a Web series, you may want a better camera that allows you to get more "professional" results. For many, the choice of camera will primarily depend on budget. However, within the range of cameras you are considering, make certain that you choose the right camera and digital video format for you. How easy is the camera to use? Does it feel right in your hands, and can you find the controls when you need them? What is the process for getting the video out of the camera and into your computer? When asking these questions, remember that it's a good idea to get a camera that is flexible enough for your future needs. While you might originally intend to produce videos solely for sites like YouTube, the videos that you produce might also be marketable on DVD or for submission to user-generated outlets, such as Current TV or even a film festival.

FIGURE 2-8   Webcams may be purchased separately or integrated into the design of your computer.

Webcams

Webcams are the most inexpensive type of camera you can buy and are widely available in any computer store or electronics retailer. While there are a variety of webcams available for Windows computers, only a few are currently available for Macs (Apple discontinued their separate iSight camera, although MacBooks and iMacs now include a built-in one). Fortunately, manufacturers are starting to see the benefit of including webcams as a package with the computers that they sell. In fact (as mentioned), it might already be built into your laptop or liquid crystal display (LCD) monitor. These cameras are great for improvised video blogs or diary reports, and can be used for other purposes, like video chats through Skype, iChat, and other applications. YouTube's QuickCapture feature takes advantage of webcams as well.

While webcams can be an extremely convenient way to capture video of yourself, they often produce notoriously low-quality images, as compared with a typical camcorder. The resolution of most webcams is relatively low; the lens is small, often made of plastic, and is sometimes so wide that it creates a characteristically distorted image. In addition, webcams require that you remain tethered to a computer, which severely limits your options for recording scenes that don't include yourself front and center. However, if you have a separately mounted webcam, you can move the camera around to get the view that you desire.

Consumer and "Prosumer" Camcorders

The range of digital video camcorders that is available today is numerous, and the choices can be daunting, even for professionals. To begin, you might want to determine whether your needs are more consumer-oriented (home use, hobbyist) or if you require more "prosumer" features (a popular term to describe professional equipment that is also within the realm of serious hobbyists). In the following sections, various aspects of camcorders are described, with suggestions that are targeted at these two groups.

Standard Definition or High Definition

Unless you've been living under a rock, you're aware that "high definition" is a popular term these days. While standard-definition video has an image size of 720 × 480 pixels (for the NTSC video standard), high-definition formats can be either 1280 × 720 pixels (720p) or 1920 × 1080 pixels (1080i or 1080p) in width and height, respectively (see Figure 2-9). Unquestionably, high-definition video offers a substantial increase in resolution (anywhere from about 2.5 to 6 times the resolution of standard-definition video), which results in clearer, more realistic images when viewed on a high-definition TV (HDTV).

So the question becomes: Is it important to buy a high-definition camcorder if I'm only creating videos for sites like YouTube? Currently, most users are creating videos for the Web and standard-definition DVDs. After all, even those with HDTVs are unable to watch their videos without outputting the video back to their camcorders. Until recordable formats for HD DVD and Blu-ray become more popular, or until devices like AppleTV become easier to use, that may be the only way. Of course, it is simply a matter of time before creating and viewing high-definition content becomes commonplace (we're getting close, especially with the capturing part). Still, at this point in time, the majority of users are creating and viewing standard-definition video.

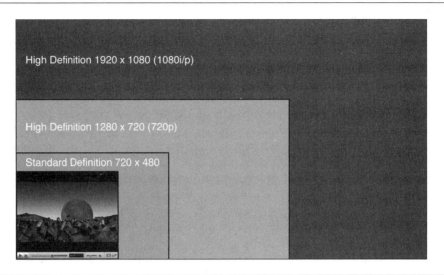

FIGURE 2-9   The difference between most Web video, standard-definition video, and high-definition video formats is dramatic.

On the other hand, most high-definition camcorders also offer the capability to record standard-definition video or to "down convert" the high-definition video they record to a standard-definition format for viewing and editing. In this case, buying a high-definition camcorder today starts to make more sense, since you are retaining all of the features of standard definition, while adding the capabilities of high-definition video for future use. This is an especially important consideration for content creators, who may want to sell or distribute their videos in the future. If you've recorded it in high definition, then you can deliver it in virtually any format, whether standard definition or high definition. Of course, the choice at present may still depend on your budget, although high-definition camcorders are now available for under $1,000, and their prices continue to drop. In addition, the computer and software that you use to capture and edit your video may limit your choices when it comes to working with certain high-definition formats, but that is a problem that is being challenged on a daily basis, with frequent software updates and more powerful computers.

Selecting a Format

In this section, a few of the most common video formats that you'll find on the market when shopping for a video camera are discussed. There are other formats not represented here, particularly higher-end formats, like DVCPROHD and XDCAM. However, the few formats discussed are representative of the primary choices facing buyers today. Ultimately, you should remember that (in most cases) while the format in which you shoot your video will be different from the output format you use to deliver your video, whether for YouTube, DVD, or other devices, it's a good idea to start with the best possible quality to achieve the best-looking results.

DV   The best standard-definition format for consumers and prosumers alike remains DV (MiniDV, DV, DVCAM, and DVCPRO all refer to essentially the same digital video format). When combined with a good camcorder, DV produces excellent results, has been used in countless documentaries and feature-film productions (including those that were transferred to film), and is supported by more video-editing software than perhaps any other format. It is an excellent choice for capturing video that will eventually make its way onto YouTube, and in its "raw" state, takes up a manageable amount of space on your hard drive (approximately 13 gigabytes [GB] per hour). If you're buying a standard-definition camcorder, this format can't be beat.

HDV   The first truly high-definition video format for consumers, HDV (high-definition video) remains a solid choice for high-quality, high-definition video at a low cost (see Figure 2-10). Somewhat maligned for its use of an MPEG-2 video compression scheme (the method used to capture and store its images), HDV is still the best compromise of quality and space for the majority of high-definition productions. Despite being a high-definition format, HDV takes up the same amount of space as DV (technically speaking, both formats have a data rate of approximately 25 megabits per second [Mbps]). In fact, HDV is usually captured and stored on the same MiniDV cassettes used by standard-definition camcorders. However, older computers may have trouble editing HDV, since its technically complex encoding scheme is harder for slower computers to decipher fast enough for playback and editing. The majority of computers sold in the last few years can handle it—just make sure to check whether your system meets the requirements listed by the manufacturer.

FIGURE 2-10   Canon has produced a popular HDV camcorder, the HV20, for consumers and aspiring filmmakers alike.

AVCHD The latest high-definition format for consumers is called AVCHD (advanced video codec high definition). Unlike most HDV camcorders, the AVCHD format is not recorded to tape and is captured to a variety of tapeless media instead (see the section "Tapeless Formats" for more information). Rather than using a type of MPEG-2 compression, like HDV uses, AVCHD utilizes a variant of the MPEG-4 (H.264) codec, which is extremely efficient and produces nearly the same results as MPEG-2 at half the data rate (the term *codec* refers to the format that compresses video for recording and decompresses it for playback). This means that you can store more video in less space than with competing high-definition formats. Support for the AVCHD format is starting to grow among video software makers, but at the time of this writing, it was still not widely supported. However, most AVCHD recordings can be played, unaltered, in a Blu-ray disc player, such as the PlayStation 3.

Tapeless Formats

Some camcorders rely on video tape to capture and store video, while others offer tapeless solutions that record to hard drives, recordable DVDs, or flash memory cards (Compact Flash, Secure Digital, or Memory Stick). The advantage to using tapeless solutions is that you have immediate access to the video data and the ability to transfer that same data to your computer in faster-than-real time. Thumbnails can be viewed in the field as you record, and clips can be instantly deleted. On the other hand, tape-based media requires that you play back and capture video on your computer in real time, and it can only be accessed in a linear fashion (fast-forward or rewind). It's like comparing a CD to cassette tape, and for that reason, many manufacturers are making the transition to tapeless devices. However, with tapeless solutions, backing up your data becomes a concern, since no physical tape exists with your media on it. Once your camera's hard drive or memory card is full, you need to delete all the data to make more space. As a result, you must be ready to buy hard drives to back up any video you want to keep (and make additional backups in case those drives fail). Still, once more high-capacity recordable media becomes available, such as recordable HD DVDs and Blu-ray discs, and with the constantly dropping prices, it's become viable to eliminate tape altogether from your video workflow. While companies like Sony, Panasonic, and Canon (to name a few) offer tapeless video recording devices, inexpensive camcorders are beginning to surface, such as those created by Flip Video, Polaroid, and others.

Single-Chip or Three-Chip Image Sensors

The vast majority of consumer camcorders includes a single image sensor to record images, which means that all colors of the visible spectrum (red, green, and blue) are captured together. On the other hand, most prosumer and professional camcorders utilize three separate image sensors, one for each color of red, green, and blue. This tends to mean that three-chip cameras produce more colorful, life-like results. In general, whether it's three CCD or three CMOS chips, three is the way to go for the best, most professional results. However, with significant advances in technology (in particular, those represented by CMOS chips in camcorders), the colors and images that are created by a good single-chip camera can be nearly indistinguishable from a three-chip counterpart. This is especially true with CMOS devices, which is the technology of choice right now, especially for high-definition camcorders.

Additional Camcorder Features

There are numerous other features that are used to sell camcorders, but the most important ones ultimately depend on your needs and the ways in which you intend to use the device. For example, it's important to many video creators that the camcorder have a microphone input and a headphone jack for recording decent audio, which is (strangely) absent from many consumer camcorders. Also, having full manual control over functions like shutter speed, aperture, and gain (topics discussed later in this chapter) is also an important consideration. In general, the ergonomics, or feel, of the camcorder are important, especially when it comes to things like focus controls, touch screens, and other everyday operations.

Accessories

The one accessory that no filmmaker should be without is a tripod. Tripods with a fluid head are best for shots that require panning or rotating the camera. However, any tripod that can adequately support the weight of your camera is better than none. A heavier tripod will keep the camera more stable, particularly if it is breezy outdoors or when touched by the operator. Still, you are more likely to carry a lighter tripod with you on a trip and when on the go.

In addition, a wide-angle adapter can be useful for shooting in tight spaces, such as cars, or even when shooting close-up in an average-size room or office. You can find a variety of optional lens attachments from different manufacturers, including "macro" lenses, but a wide-angle adapter is generally the most useful.

You should also pick up an ultraviolet (UV) filter for protecting your lens from dirt and scratches. It's always better to replace a cheap filter than try to fix the built-in lens on your camcorder. For serious enthusiasts, consider additional filter types, such as ND (neutral density) filters, which reduce the amount of light that enters the lens (useful when shooting in bright conditions) or polarizing filters, which reduce glare and reflections from glass, as well as producing bluer skies.

Operating Your Camcorder

Although you don't have to be Steven Spielberg to create a video for YouTube, it will certainly help the quality of your video if you apply some basic filmmaking principles to the process of creating your YouTube videos. To begin, you'll learn about using a camcorder and then explore some of the compositions that you can create. While the general operation of a camcorder, such as turning it on, inserting a tape, and other types of controls are not discussed in this chapter (those are better left to your chosen camcorder's instructional manual), some of the issues that result from working with a camera are covered here.

Holding the Camcorder

Use a tripod whenever possible! Nothing is a replacement for the solid foundation that a tripod provides. If you do find it necessary to move the camera, make sure that you do it deliberately and as smoothly as possible. Make your movements slow, and keep the camera in line with the horizon (do not rotate the camera). When holding the camera in a stationary position, keep your legs far enough apart to provide a stable base. Place your right hand through the side grip of the camera, and keep your right elbow against your body. Use your other hand to help steady the camera.

In addition, if you must hold your camera, make sure that the camera's image-stabilization feature is activated. Image stabilization in a camera simply makes your shots appear steadier by removing some of the minor bumps and jitter that are associated with holding a camera. On Sony's camcorders, this feature is referred to as SteadyShot, and on Canon's camcorders it's called OIS (optical image stabilization). This feature should already be turned on by default, and will likely be a part of any automatic mode that you choose. The only time you would want to turn this feature off is when the camera is mounted on a tripod. The image-stabilization feature on a camera may cause the image to drift or glide slightly, which is something that you want to avoid when using a tripod. Even the slightest vibration may cause the stabilizer to kick in when it is not necessary.

Focusing

While automatic focus is not always accurate, it is, by far, the simplest method and is probably adequate for most nonprofessional usage (although, David Lynch apparently made extensive use of it in his DV-shot movie *Inland Empire*). When using the automatic focus on your camera, it is best to avoid changing lighting conditions, especially in low-light situations, where it's difficult for the camera to lock on to a subject. Also, try to maintain a constant distance from your subject whenever possible to avoid refocusing. In general, make sure to reduce the amount of change in the frame, such as people walking by the lens, the headlights of passing cars, or other movement that will cause the camera to search for new focus. This searching for focus is sometimes referred to as *hunting*, and is the camera's attempt to lock its focus on to a subject. This can happen even when a camera is set up on a tripod.

To avoid unwanted shifts in focus, you must use manual focus. Manual focus is the preferred method for professional results. It provides you with greater artistic control and allows for precise adjustments. One situation where manual focus is particularly useful is when subjects are placed at different distances from the camera. For example, you can use manual focus to focus on a person standing in the background, even if there is someone else in the foreground. If you were to use automatic focus, it would almost certainly choose the person closer to the camera to focus on. Other situations where manual focus is preferable include low-light situations, when there is a lot of motion in the frame (people or objects that move quickly are difficult for automatic focus to lock on to), subjects are walking into or out of the frame, or extremely bright-light sources that are pointed at the camera (such as spotlights, lamps, or even the sun).

When using manual focus, the best way to make sure you are focusing correctly is to zoom in to your subject as close as possible, adjust the focus until the subject is sharp, and then zoom back out to reframe the shot. From this point forward, regardless of where you place the zoom control (near or far), the subject will be in focus—that is, until you or the subject moves, of course. Some prosumer cameras will also include a "push focus" button that temporarily utilizes the camera's automatic focus controls to lock on to a subject, returning to manual control as soon as the button is released. This may be an effective method for making use of the best features of both manual and automatic focus. Again, for general use, automatic focus is still the simplest and (depending on the capabilities of the camera) can produce surprising results.

Zooming

If you want your video to look professional, avoid zooming while shooting. Instead, use zooms only to reframe a shot, particularly when shooting from a distance. On most cameras, the zoom controls are indicated with a "W" for wide shots and a "T" for tight shots. Use the zoom ring or the zoom rocker on your camera before, not while, shooting a shot. Zooming during a shot draws undue attention and, in most cases, looks amateurish. Of course, there are times when a zooming motion is useful, such as when you want to achieve a slow "crawling" effect (as if the camera was slowly, almost imperceptibly, moving closer to the subject). In any case, it's best to avoid sudden zooming, unless you're shooting a kung fu parody. Also, always avoid using the low-quality digital zoom on your camcorder. Digital zooms are a marketing ploy, which simply produce a digital scaling effect that degrades the quality of your image, similar to scaling an image past its native resolution in Photoshop.

Adjusting Exposure

Exposure is the trickiest set of controls to adjust on any camera. In fact, there are three possible controls that affect the exposure of an image: shutter, aperture (iris), and gain (sensitivity). When a camera is placed in full auto mode, it will set all of these controls for you automatically, even when faced with changing lighting conditions. However, there are many times (especially during professional use) where having manual control over exposure can be not only useful, but downright necessary.

These days, most cameras are fairly smart when it comes to analyzing and making settings for you. Still, cameras do not always make the right choices, and for consistent, reliable results, manually adjusting exposure is often the best way. For example, a camera that is set on automatic may change exposure in the middle of a shot when someone passes through the frame or when you point the camera in a slightly different direction than the last, possibly triggering a change in exposure (the camera continually attempts to make the best overall exposure). Putting the camera in full manual mode to adjust exposure (if your camera is capable of it) allows you to make a single setting that stays exactly where you want until you tell it otherwise. Now, you can set the proper shutter, aperture, and gain settings for a given scene, and your video will appear similarly and properly exposed for that situation.

In general, when making manual adjustments to exposure on the fly, it is best to leave your camera set at a given shutter speed (usually 1/60 second for NTSC) and then adjust aperture independently as needed. While the implications of setting shutter speeds and aperture are somewhat complex (affecting "depth of field," for instance), it is most important to know that the aperture (or iris) is the hole that controls the amount of light that's let into the camera, while shutter speed determines how long that hole remains open. A shutter speed of 1/60 of a second closely matches the 30 frames (60 fields) of video for NTSC, and so it appears most natural, although faster shutter speeds may be better for action scenes to eliminate motion blur. In low-light situations, a wide open aperture (F 1.8, for example) is useful, along with a slower shutter speed (1/60 is the lowest you'd usually want to go for NTSC without introducing too much motion blur). Gain, on the other hand, is an artificial increase in the sensitivity of the video capture, which can be useful for capturing images in very low light, while also introducing the significant problem of video "noise," which looks similar to grain in film. Usually, for professional results, it's best to turn the gain off completely or at least set it very low, if necessary. If you're interested in learning more about photographic principles, it's worthwhile to study some books on still photography or professional video capture, which address the many complexities of getting proper image exposure.

Setting Up a Shot

The following section describes some basic filmmaking terms that are used to illustrate the elements of good video composition. This is only a cursory examination of the elements that can be combined to create an interesting video for YouTube, and is a point of departure for those interested in exploring film and video concepts on their own.

Shot Types

There are a variety of ways that you can describe the composition of an image. However, in the language of film and video, certain basic terms are applied to describe the size of a subject within the frame. In fact, there are several more subcategories that are not listed in this section, but this should give a brief introduction to the types of shots that will help you to compose images for YouTube videos.

Wide Shot (or Long Shot)

A wide shot (WS) frames action from a distance, and is useful for shooting an "establishing shot" that often comes at the beginning of a sequence (setting up the locale, as it were). However, wide shots are generally not very useful for video created for the Web, since they produce too much detail that is difficult to see when looking at the picture on a computer screen, particularly when the video is played in a window that is used for presenting Web video. For this reason, it's best to avoid wide shots except where absolutely necessary to establish a location or setting.

Full Shot

A full shot (FS) is framed to include the entire subject, such as a person from head to toe. It's basically another type of long shot, except the framing is generally tighter than a wide shot. Again, it's not the most useful type of shot for Web video, but can be used when needed to establish the scale of a character.

Medium Shot

A medium shot (MS) is usually framed from the waist or chest up, including the subject's head (see Figure 2-11). Medium shots are particularly useful when you want to reveal the gestures that a subject makes, since the arms and torso are easy to see. Medium shots are good for Web video, since they reveal enough of the subject to tell a story, while reducing unnecessary details in the background.

Close-up

Perhaps, the most useful and relevant type of shot for Web video is a close-up (CU), since it frames the subject closer to the viewer and reveals much more information within a limited space. When shooting people, close-ups are generally framed from the neck or slightly lower up, including the head. The person's face is the featured subject in the frame (see Figure 2-11). This type of shot is also used to show details of hands, feet, or other objects where you want to highlight certain attributes (extreme close-ups are a variation on this type of shot that move the camera even closer). In addition, close-ups will generally help your video compress better for the Web by reducing the appearance of complex backgrounds and keeping the important elements prominently in the frame. They will also look better than any other shot within a small, video player window, like the player on YouTube.

Angles and Camera Height

In addition to the size of your subject within the frame, the angle and height of the camera have a noticeable impact on the images that you create. In this section, we cover the most common shots that you will use. Varying the placement and orientation of your camera can create interesting looks, depending on the effect you are trying to achieve.

FIGURE 2-11   Medium shots and close-ups work well for YouTube and the Web in general.

Eye Level

Just as it sounds, placing a camera at eye level helps the viewer communicate more directly with the subject. This is probably the type of shot you will use most often in your YouTube videos, particularly if you are creating a video blog or talking directly to the camera.

High Angle

High angles are shots that are performed looking down at a subject from a high perspective, such as from on top of a ladder, chair, or tall building. These shots can create dramatic impact, particularly when you want to make a character look weaker or to give an omniscient point of view. On YouTube, you often see a slightly more subtle version of this camera angle when people use a webcam placed on top of their computer to film themselves.

Low Angle

Low angles are shots that look up at a subject from below, such as from the ground. These shots make someone look taller or more menacing, while making the viewer feel small or insignificant. You often see these in horror movies to portray the villain. Unless you're making a short film or skit, you may not use this one very often, although it can be useful for giving a sense of scale when shooting a tall building.

Oblique Angle

An oblique angle is simply an angle that is tilted to create an unusual, sometimes unsettling, perspective. While not used often, an oblique (also called a "dutch") angle can make the framing more interesting or communicate a sense of instability for a character.

TIP

In addition to the shots mentioned in this section, consider placing your camera at unusual camera heights to capture the perspective of a child or pet (low to the ground), or from a kneeling position, where you can make your images a little less bland, particularly if shooting outdoors. Experiment with ways to make your images stand out.

Principles for Framing Your Subject

Now that you've taken a look at a variety of shot types, angles, and camera positions, it is time to put these ideas into practice. But first, it's important to note that simply composing an image in a close-up, for example, can mean different things to different people. To achieve optimal results (results that are widely perceived as "correct" or pleasing), there are a few additional principles relating to image composition that must be considered.

The first of these principles is called the "rule of thirds." The idea behind the rule of thirds is that a frame can be divided into nine parts (three vertical sections and three horizontal sections) by drawing two vertical lines and two horizontal lines equally spaced across the frame (see Figure 2-12). As a result, a strong point of interest is created at the intersection of two lines. By aligning features to one of those points, a more interesting composition is created. For example,

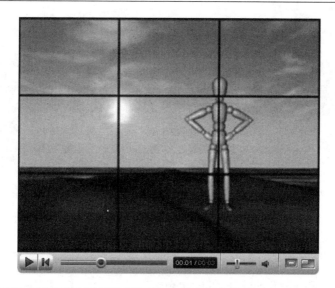

FIGURE 2-12   The "rule of thirds" is a useful technique for finding pleasing compositions.

placing a subject's eyes at that point can create a strong composition. In addition, when shooting a landscape shot, it is usually best to place the horizon at either the bottom or top third of the frame, with any significant features placed at the intersection of lines in the left or right third of the frame. While it frequently results in nice compositions, the rule of thirds, like any other "rule" discussed here, is simply a rough compositional tool to help you make decisions while shooting.

Another principle to consider when shooting a short film is referred to as the "180 degree rule," which directly relates to your subject's screen direction. Simply put, when filming a scene, an imaginary line can be drawn through each subject, connecting them to each other. Keeping the camera on the correct side of that line (the side that you establish at the beginning of the scene) means that your screen direction will stay consistent and not create confusion. This is particularly important when shooting a conversation between two or more people, where each party is facing the other in opposing directions. For example, in a conversation between two people, subject A may be facing to the right, while subject B may be facing to the left. It is important that in all the shots you shoot for this sequence, regardless of shot type (close-up, full shot, etc.), that this same right-to-left relationship is maintained, thus sustaining the illusion when the shots are eventually edited together that the spatial relationship is correct (see Figure 2-13). Consequently, subject A is always facing right and subject B is always facing left. Leaving sufficient "nose room," or negative space, in front of each person's face is useful to set up this sort of spatial relationship as well, and it also looks better when composing shots (this also relates to the rule of thirds). Screen direction is equally important when filming a subject that moves through the frame, such

Chad Vader - Day Shift Manager (episode 1)

FIGURE 2-13 It's important to maintain screen direction when shooting a scene.

as when an actor leaves through a door. If in the first shot they move to exit on the right, they should be filmed in the next shot leaving on the right.

With the advent of digital television and HDTV, another issue arises for videos that we create for YouTube. While YouTube is currently limited to video images with a 4:3 aspect ratio, many users may have images that originated at a widescreen 16:9 aspect ratio. In Chapter 3, we discuss how to prepare widescreen video for uploading to YouTube by first "letterboxing" the video.

Camera Movement

As discussed earlier, camera movement should be smooth and deliberate. Most often, camera movements are performed from a tripod, but the same types of moves discussed in this section apply to handheld motion as well. However, for Web video, motions like panning and tilting are not generally recommended, at least when you want to avoid adding to the "complexity" of a shot, thus increasing the difficulty for video encoders to apply compression (the video that is processed before it can be viewed easily online). Take that last word of caution with a grain of salt, however, since camera movement is part of the art of creating dynamic and interesting videos, and it may be worth the effort.

Panning and Tilting

Panning is the motion that is produced by turning a camera smoothly about its center axis from side to side. This is a useful motion for taking in a landscape or other scene that is too large to be seen well in a single shot. It can also be used to follow a subject as he or she moves through the scene. Although using a tripod is strongly recommended, you can also pan with a handheld camera by twisting your body at the waist. Keep your feet firmly planted, and pivot your body slowly. For the most pleasing results, pan very slowly, which will also reduce the amount of motion blur that is produced. Titling is simply an up or down variation on a pan, which can be used to show the size of a tall building by tilting up (for example) or to reveal the entrance of a subject into your scene.

Dolly

Physically moving the camera closer or farther away from a subject in a smooth motion is called a dolly move. This is a useful type of camera movement for following a subject forward or backward through a scene or for surveying the landscape in a smooth lateral motion. You can do this with a camera that is mounted on a wheeled cart running on tracks (the long-favored professional method used in many films), with a Steadicam type of device, or by simply holding the camera while walking carefully. If you choose to hold your camcorder while performing this type of move, use two hands, make sure to watch your flipout viewscreen, and try to hold the camcorder as steady as possible, as if it were floating in space.

Lighting Your Subject

Although the average consumer or low-budget indie may not have the money for expensive lights, there are plenty of things you can do to improve the lighting of your subject that costs nothing or very little. However, if you do plan on producing independent films, particularly of the fictional variety, you should considering investing in a modest light kit or borrowing the gear that you might need for a particular shoot.

As with any other aspect of shooting a video, the environment that you choose to record in can have a dramatic effect on the results that you achieve. First, when choosing a location for a subject that you want to light, avoid placing the subject with his or her back to a window. Your camera will adjust exposure to compensate for the light coming through the window (the brightest light source in the scene), and your subject will appear dark and underexposed. To avoid this, place your subject opposite the window or at a pleasing angle where he or she can catch the light on his or her face. When shooting outdoors, it is also best to have the sun shining toward your subject, not from behind or directly above. If the light source (in this case, the sun) is shining directly down on a person, long, dark shadows will be cast under the eyes. The only way to solve these lighting conditions is to shoot at a different time of day (avoid shooting around noon) or to use additional lights and reflectors to compensate by casting more light on the subject where needed.

Ideally, you are able to control the light that is cast on your subject by adding the light sources yourself. A "key" light can be added as the primary light source that shines on your subject's face to illuminate the most important features and make it bright enough to be seen clearly on camera. This light may be a professional hard or soft light source (*hard* and *soft* refer to the quality of the light), such as you can find in a photography store. An additional "fill" light, which is most often a soft and less directional light, may be added to eliminate shadows and fill in areas that are opposite the portions illuminated by the key light.

In fact, there are many ways that lights of many sorts can be used to reveal features in a scene—far more than we could ever cover here. Just remember that it's important to light a subject so that you can see their face clearly and so that they are separated adequately from the background. This might even mean using a work lamp that you buy at a hardware store or simply placing your subject next to a house lamp in the living room.

Light has different colors, depending on its "temperature." Outdoor light is bluer, while indoor light is generally more orange. Your camcorder usually does a decent job of setting the white balance to properly compensate for the light that it captures. However, if you see a blue or orange cast to your video, you might want to manually set the white balance for your camera. In fact, the white balance is an important feature to set anyway for professional results that accurately match the light present in a scene. Manually select an indoor or outdoor lighting preset, or point your camera at a white surface, such as a sheet of paper or wall, and press the white balance button (consult your camera's manual for specific instructions).

Recording Flawless Audio

Audio is probably the most overlooked aspect of any video production. When recording audio along with your video, make sure that you capture audio that is easily discernable and free from unnecessary noise. Generally speaking, there are two ways you can record better audio. The first is to control the environment in which you are recording, and the second is to select the right equipment for the job.

When choosing where to record your video, consider how the location will affect the audio. Select a location that is free from background noise, such as air conditioners, ventilation systems, cars, airplanes, and other traffic or city noise. If possible, also try to record in a room without a lot of reverb or reflection off of surfaces, such as auditoriums or other places that produce an echo. Always make sure to wear headphones to judge the quality of the audio your camera is capturing and to properly judge audio levels.

With regard to audio-recording devices, the microphone on your camcorder is most often the worst microphone for the job. If you want to record high-quality audio, you need to use a microphone that is designed for the task. The microphone that is built into a camcorder is not only of low quality (one of the areas a manufacturer cuts corners), it is also designed to pick up sound in all directions (omnidirectional). This means that the audio captured by the camera not only includes the voice you may want to record, but also all the environmental sounds coming from the sides. When you are recording someone's voice, you want it to stand out from all other sounds. In order to capture what is immediately in front of your camera, you should use a separate directional microphone.

A short shotgun microphone is designed for this purpose (see Figure 2-14), as long as the subject is within a few feet. Despite its name and dimensions, a shotgun microphone is not designed to capture audio at a long distance, only within a narrow range in front of the microphone, thus eliminating excess noise from the side or behind. You can purchase shotgun microphones that sit on top of your camera's accessory shoe or that can be held with special "boom" poles. For most users, mounting a shotgun microphone on top of your camera is easiest.

A lavalier microphone is even better for recording only the voices that you want to hear, reducing extraneous noise more than any other microphone. This is due to the proximity that a lavalier microphone has to the speaker's mouth. Lavalier microphones are small, and are most often clipped onto a subject's clothing, midway up their chest or closer to the collar. In fact,

FIGURE 2-14   A shotgun microphone is a good replacement for a camcorder's on-camera microphone.

lavalier microphones can be positioned other places (like a pant leg or sleeve) to get appropriate foley sounds, such as footsteps. You can purchase wired or wireless lavalier microphones, depending on the needs (and budget) of your production.

In addition, you can use a standard handheld microphone, which is particularly useful if you are conducting interviews with people on the street or when it's impractical to work with lavaliers. It's likely that you will need an adapter to connect a handheld microphone, such as a Shure SM58 or similar device, to your camcorder if you don't have the proper inputs. Most consumer camcorders that have a microphone input usually have a mini-jack, not the XLR connections preferred by professional audio gear.

Shooting Video That Looks Good When Uploaded to YouTube

Unfortunately, there is no single secret to creating video that looks good once it's uploaded to YouTube. In fact, it is a combination of factors that contribute to pleasing results. Many of the techniques scattered throughout this chapter are a start. For example, it is helpful to reduce the complexity of your video to make it compress better when it is encoded for YouTube. Reducing the complexity of the image starts with choosing a simple background, with little or no motion in it (such as a solid-colored background), with a video camera that is placed on a tripod or in another stationary position (a webcam attached to a computer monitor, for instance), utilizing tight compositions, such as close-ups, and video that is lit brightly and exposed correctly to reduce "noise" in the image (turn off the gain if possible). In the end, though, it's important that these "rules" for producing simple images that compress well for YouTube do not limit your creativity. Compression schemes for the Web continue to improve, and even videos that compress poorly will find an audience, as long as the imagination of their creators continues to shine through.

Chapter 3

Editing Your Videos

How to...

- Understand the editing workflow
- Select the best editing software for your needs
- Work with Windows Movie Maker
- Work with iMovie
- Think about editing creatively
- Use YouTube's AudioSwap
- Use YouTube's Remixer

Once you've acquired video using a camera, as discussed in the last chapter, it's time to put the pieces together and create a finished movie. Of course, if your video consists of a single shot, then "editing" might not be applicable. However, you still need to capture the video onto your computer, and even a video blog or diary entry can be polished a bit with the addition of titles, a color effect, or some music or sound effects. In this chapter, you will learn about a variety of techniques and YouTube features that will help you to produce a more interesting video.

Understanding Basic Editing Principles

For those who are new to working with video, particularly those without previous multimedia experience, the process of editing and outputting a movie might seem intimidating. However, most video creators follow a simple workflow that is relevant to virtually any production, whether amateur or professional. In general, basic editing principles are universal and part of any software package that you choose. Obviously, the more advanced applications will expand on these principles by offering additional options and tools. Still, for most people creating videos for YouTube, editing is meant to be a casual, enjoyable endeavor. The first step is to capture or import the video that you want to work with. The actual steps to accomplish this task depend on the video format and media that you used to record the video, as well as the software that you have on your computer. Most often, the process involves connecting your camcorder to a computer using a special FireWire or Universal Serial Bus (USB) cable, although analog video connections and newer digital connections, such as High Definition Multimedia Interface (HDMI) are available in certain cases. Then you use the software to control the playback and transfer of material from the videotape or disc in the device to your Mac or PC. Your captured video appears within a browser, or bin, inside your editing software. In most cases, you will use the same application to capture and edit your video, which simplifies the entire video creation process. The video media is now stored on your hard drive, and the editing software maintains links that reference the captured media.

At this point, the video resides on your computer and you can begin to edit. You will use the tools in your video-editing software to assemble your video clips as a coherent sequence by setting in and out points for each clip (which determines how much of the clip is actually used) and then placing them into a timeline that represents a linear arrangement of clips. This is the creative part of the equation. The simplest movies on YouTube, as well as feature-length films, use the same process to construct their narratives. In addition to piecing together these blocks of video, you can incorporate additional audio tracks at this stage (such as music, sound effects, and voice-overs), still photos and graphics, text for titles, transitions between clips, and special effects to enhance the look of your production.

Once you've created a movie out of the building blocks provided by your video clips, soundtracks, and graphics, you can output your finished piece to share with the world. This part of the process can be done in a variety of ways, depending on where the piece will finally be shown. For example, you can output your video to a DVD, as a video podcast accessible through iTunes, or as a file that can be uploaded to YouTube. Of course, for the purposes of our discussion, the latter option is likely the one you will choose. In Chapter 4, you will learn how to prepare your video for uploading to YouTube, as well as some tips to optimize it for the best-looking results.

Choosing Your Editing Software

Before you start to assemble your video masterpiece, you must have software that allows you to work with the video clips you have recorded. In general, the software discussed in this chapter is designed for beginners to use and comes preinstalled on your operating system of choice (Mac or PC). For more advanced users and serious hobbyists, additional software choices are discussed in this section as well.

Video-Editing Software for PCs

For many PC users, Windows Movie Maker is sufficient for creating videos for YouTube, although some may find this software lacking in features. For that reason, you may want to consider a variety of other software options if you intend to do a lot of editing for your YouTube videos.

Windows Movie Maker

Most computers running the Windows XP (Service Pack 2) or Windows Vista operating system should have Windows Movie Maker already installed. This application is Microsoft's entry into the field of easy-to-use editing software for PC users. Editing and effects features in Windows Movie Maker are fairly basic (see Figure 3-1), but you can augment it with add-ons from companies like Pixelan and others. You can check out more about Windows Movie Maker, including additional tutorials, at www.microsoft.com/windowsxp/using/moviemaker.

TIP   *It's almost always a good idea to use the latest edition of your editing software, particularly if you want access to the newest features and functionality. To check which version of Windows Movie Maker you are running, start the application, click the Help menu drop-down arrow, and choose About Windows Movie Maker to check the version number. You can find the latest software downloads by visiting www.microsoft.com/ downloads.*

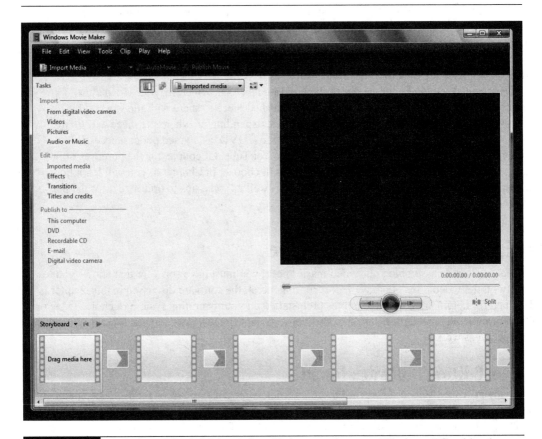

FIGURE 3-1 Windows Movie Maker is installed on nearly every Windows PC sold today.

Adobe Premiere Elements

For users that demand better control and more features in their editing software, Adobe (makers of the ubiquitous Photoshop, After Effects, and other well-known applications) has created an entry-level video-editing application called Premiere Elements (see Figure 3-2). Premiere Elements is basically a stripped-down version of Adobe's high-end editing software (and more expensive) Premiere Pro. For most users, Premiere Elements will meet their needs, with an interface that is straightforward and easy to use. For more information about Adobe Premiere Elements, visit www.adobe.com/products/premiereel.

Adobe Premiere Pro (PC and Mac)

Once you're ready to move into more advanced projects and editing, Adobe offers Premiere Pro, a more full-featured and professional application with few limitations (see Figure 3-3).

FIGURE 3-2   Adobe Premiere Elements is a good place to start for beginners, and is a step up from Windows Movie Maker.

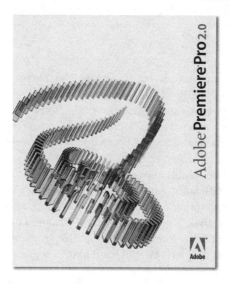

FIGURE 3-3   Adobe Premiere Pro is a great choice for professional editing on either a Mac or a PC.

Premiere Pro also comes with OnLocation, a live monitoring solution when shooting in the field with a laptop, as well as Adobe Encore DVD authoring application. In fact, Adobe now offers a variety of packages that include Premiere Pro along with a variety of other software products that you might find useful. When you've reached your limit with Premiere Elements, consider moving up to Premiere Pro. Premiere Pro has been around for many years, and was one of the first serious editing applications for both Macs and PCs. After many years of supporting both platforms, Premiere Pro became a PC-only application. However, with the latest version of the software, Premiere Pro is once again available for both Macs and PCs, although it still faces stiff competition from Final Cut Pro for the Mac. You can read more about the features in Premiere Pro at www.adobe.com/products/premiere.

Additional Editing Software

As the most widely supported platform for computer software and hardware, it's no surprise that there is a virtually endless supply of video applications for the PC. Some of the most popular alternatives to the ones mentioned here are Avid Xpress and Sony Vegas, as well as products by Ulead, Pinnacle (currently owned by Avid), and others. In terms of professional results, editing systems by Avid, including Xpress DV and Xpress Pro, can't be beat, especially on the PC (its closest competitor is Final Cut Pro for the Mac). Check out www.avid.com for more information. It's possible that the camera you purchased or the computer you bought also came preinstalled with additional software for working with video.

Video-Editing Software for the Mac

One of the great things about a Mac is that it comes preconfigured with a variety of really useful software, such as the iLife suite of multimedia applications. However, if you require more control over the videos that you create, there are more advanced options for both hobbyists and professionals alike.

iMovie

iMovie is just one of the iLife applications that ships with every Mac (see Figure 3-4). The applications in iLife include iMovie, iDVD, iPhoto, GarageBand, iWeb, and the freely available iTunes. Since they are all part of the same suite, the applications in iLife work together seamlessly, allowing you to easily move media from one application to another. For example, you can move pictures from iPhoto and songs captured in iTunes or created in GarageBand to iMovie with a few mouse clicks. The layout of the application is straightforward as well, and even the complete novice will be making movies in a matter of minutes. In fact, while iMovie is by far the simplest editing application for the Mac (or perhaps any other computer system, for that matter), it can produce surprising results. A few years ago, a director named Jonathan Caouette even made a feature-length documentary called *Tarnation* using iMovie that earned praise at festivals like Sundance. Many YouTubers rely on iMovie everyday to quickly assemble their videos as well. Later in this chapter, you will learn how to begin a new project in iMovie.

FIGURE 3-4   iMovie is part of the iLife suite that is installed on all Apple computers.

Check out www.apple.com/ilife for the latest information about iMovie and the other iLife applications.

Final Cut Express

Final Cut Express represents a major step upward from iMovie in terms of the ability to work with video clips in a more professional manner (see Figure 3-5). Rather than being limited to single tracks for video and audio media, you can create nearly limitless tracks and use more advanced tools to trim and edit your clips. You can also perform more advanced motion effects with "keyframing," basic color correction, and other features demanded by professionals. In fact, it's suggested that if you want better control over the editing process in general, Final Cut Express is a great entry point, particularly for film students that are looking to one day advance to a career in the industry. Apple frequently offers deals on Final Cut Express software with the purchase of a new Mac, not to mention the educational pricing that is available for students and faculty of grade schools, high schools, colleges, and universities. Currently, Final Cut Express supports editing with just two video formats, DV and HDV, although (like any other software out there) format compatibility changes over time. Check out www.apple.com/finalcutexpress for updates and more information.

FIGURE 3-5   Final Cut Express is a good choice for students and video-makers who want to take a step up from iMovie to a more professional application.

Final Cut Pro

For professional video creators working on a Mac, the preferred choice for editing software is Final Cut Pro (see Figure 3-6). Final Cut Pro comes bundled with a suite called Final Cut Studio containing other, highly capable and professional applications, which will also be of interest to editors, animators, producers, and directors working in the field of video production. Final Cut Studio consists of Final Cut Pro, DVD Studio Pro, Motion, Soundtrack Pro, Color, Compressor, and DVD Studio Pro. Like the iLife suite, all of the Final Cut Studio applications work phenomenally well together, making it easy to transition between all stages of post-production. In particular, Final Cut Pro acts as the hub around which every editing tool imaginable is at your disposal. While it may seem like overkill for an average YouTube project, once you've become familiar with the workings of an application like Final Cut Pro, it's possible to create videos that can be shown not only on YouTube, but also anywhere that professional videos are exhibited. In addition, Final Cut Pro offers the widest compatibility when it comes to different video formats, which is particularly important if you are working with the latest cameras or somewhat obscure formats. Check out www.apple.com/finalcutstudio for updates and more information.

FIGURE 3-6   Final Cut Pro (part of the Final Cut Studio suite) is often preferred by professionals who work in the video production and film industries.

Capturing and Editing Your Video Using Windows Movie Maker

If your computer is running Windows, then it's highly likely that it was preconfigured with Windows Movie Maker. In this section, we briefly discuss the process for beginning a new project and editing it with Windows Movie Maker. In Chapter 4, outputting your videos for YouTube using Movie Maker is discussed in detail.

Starting a New Project and Capturing Video with Windows Movie Maker

When beginning a new project, you should first choose a location in which to store it. The following steps demonstrate how to set up a new project for Windows Movie Maker:

1. Start Windows Movie Maker by choosing Start | All Programs | Windows Movie Maker (if your application has been moved to another folder on the Start menu, locate it there). Alternately, you can just hook up a video camera to your computer and then choose

Capture Video Using Windows Movie Maker if prompted with the Digital Video Device dialog box, followed by and clicking OK. If your camera is recognized right away, you may also just see the Video Capture Wizard and can skip ahead to step 4.

2. Once the application opens, choose File | Save Project As, and then choose a location on your hard drive to store the new project file (which will also include the video that you capture in subsequent steps), and then click Save.

3. With your video camera connected, click the From Digital Video Camera link under the Import Tasks area on the left side of the interface (if this area is not visible, click the Tasks button near the top of the interface). The Video Capture Wizard should open with the first page of the wizard, called Captured Video File, displayed.

4. Type a name for the video file you are about to capture in the first text field, and choose a location to store your captured videos by selecting it from the drop-down menu in the area underneath (the default location is My Videos).

5. Click Next to proceed to the Capture Method page of the Video Capture Wizard.

6. Select Capture The Entire Tape Automatically or Capture Parts Of The Tape Manually. As noted, if you choose the first option, the video tape rewinds to the beginning and the video is then captured automatically. If you choose the second option, you will need to cue the video tape to the part of the video you want to capture and start the capture process manually. You can capture more than one part of the video tape without restarting the wizard. At this point, you should click Next, and follow the instructions for the particular option you have chosen.

TIP *You can set up your preferences for a project by choosing Tools | Options and then adjusting settings on the Advanced tab (such as NTSC or PAL, 4:3 or 16:9).*

Editing Video with Windows Movie Maker

Once you've captured video with Windows Movie Maker, you are ready to start editing. The following steps demonstrate the most basic procedure for working with clips in Movie Maker and editing them into the timeline to create a sequence.

1. Drag a video clip from the browser into the timeline at the bottom of the Windows Movie Maker interface.

2. Continue to drag clips from the browser to the timeline to construct a complete sequence of clips. Notice that you can view a sequence of clips as a timeline or as a storyboard by clicking either Show Timeline or Show Storyboard. This is similar to working in iMovie with the Clip Viewer or Timeline Viewer modes. Both modes accomplish the same thing for simple sequences (the timeline view simply offers more options for trimming and manipulating video and audio). Once you have at least two clips in the timeline, you might consider adding a transition between them, as discussed in the following steps.

3. Choose Tools | Transitions from the menu at the top of the screen.

4. Scroll down the Transitions window, locate a transition that you like, and drag the transition between two clips in the timeline or storyboard view. Notice that there are a large number of possible transitions available.

5. Click the Play Storyboard or Play Timeline button to preview your sequence.

Capturing and Editing Your Video Using iMovie

As mentioned earlier, if the computer you're working with is a Mac, then you are fortunate to have iMovie (and the other iLife applications) already installed. Of course, if you are working on an older Macintosh computer, you may want to upgrade your iLife suite to the latest version in order to take advantage of the tools that it offers. Apple is known for introducing software that is both easy to use and full of features that are fun and powerful. You can check out www.apple.com/ilife for more information about the latest version and the benefits it offers. Using iMovie is a snap and should take even a die-hard PC user no time to learn.

Starting a New Project and Capturing Video with iMovie

The following steps demonstrate the basic procedure for setting up a new iMovie project and capturing video prior to the start of editing your clips together.

1. Start iMovie by clicking its shortcut icon in the dock or by locating its application icon in the Applications folder.

2. When the iMovie start screen appears, click the Create A New Project button to proceed with creating a new project.

3. In the Create Project dialog box that appears, type a name for your project, choose a location to save it (the default is your Movies folder), and click Create. A new project file is created, and the iMovie interface is displayed.

4. Click the Switch To Capture Mode button (it looks like a camcorder and is located to the left of the scissors icon), which enables the video capture mode of iMovie. At this point, you should see a blue viewer window with the words "Video Camera." If a camera or video deck is not properly connected to your Mac, you will see a message that says "No Camera Attached."

5. Use the playback controls under the viewer window to play, fast-forward, and rewind your videotape to the point where you want to start capturing.

6. Click the Import button to begin capturing video from your camcorder to your computer. New clips are automatically made any time scene-break information is detected, which is based on wherever you started and stopped the tape while recording (assuming you set the time and date information on your camcorder). You can deactivate this feature if you want to capture a single long clip, although this isn't usually necessary. If you decide to deactivate this feature, choose iMovie | Preferences, click the Import button, and clear

the Start A New Clip At Each Scene Break option prior to capturing your video. You can also break up clips manually after they've been captured, which is often the most reliable method.

7. When you are ready to stop capturing, click the Import button again or press the ESC key on your keyboard to end the capture process. Notice that all of the video you captured can be seen in the browser window on the right of the interface, with separate clips created whenever there was new time and date information on your camcorder.

Editing Video with iMovie

Once you've captured some video with iMovie, you are ready to start editing. The following steps demonstrate the basic procedure for working with clips in iMovie and editing them into the timeline to create a sequence. This exercise represents only a fraction of what you can do with iMovie, but should get you off to a good start working with the application.

1. Click the Switch To Edit Mode button (it looks like a camcorder and is located to the right of the camcorder icon), which enables the video edit mode of iMovie.

2. Click a clip in the browser on the right to view the clip in the viewer on the left. You can click the Play button underneath the viewer to watch your clip.

3. Set in and out points for your clip in the viewer (points that signify where the clip should start and stop playing back, respectively, which determines how much of the clip you actually want to use) by dragging the appropriate triangular in and out point indicators underneath your video. As you move the in and out point indicators, the playhead moves with them, showing your current location in the clip. The area of the clip that you want to keep is now highlighted, with in and out points on either side.

4. When you are ready to set these in and out points permanently and remove the extra media on either side, choose Edit | Crop. Cropping clips is a procedure that is unique to an entry-level application like iMovie, since more professional applications (like Final Cut Express and Final Cut Pro) allow you to easily keep the clip information intact, while still making use of in and out points.

5. Click the Add And Arrange Video Clips In The Clip Viewer button on the left side of the interface, located above the timeline (it's the button that looks like a film frame to the left of the button with a clock icon).

6. Drag the clip from the browser to the timeline at the bottom of the interface. The clip that you dragged to the timeline is removed from the browser and now only exists in the timeline. This means that you can only use a clip once, unless you copy it first (using the Edit | Copy and Edit | Paste commands). While common for entry-level editing software, the removal of a clip from the browser is different from what you would find in an application like Final Cut Express or Final Cut Pro, which allows you to easily reuse clips and edit them nondestructively.

7. Continue to drag clips from the browser to the timeline to construct a complete sequence of clips. Once you have at least two clips in the timeline, you might consider adding a transition between them, as discussed in the following steps.

8. Click the Editing button under the clip browser to open the Editing pane, which contains all of the possible titles, transitions, and special effects you can add to your videos. For this exercise, you'll simply add a transition between clips.

9. Click the Transitions button at the top of the Editing pane, and locate a transition that you like. One of the most common transitions is the cross dissolve, which transitions one clip smoothly into the other without fading to black.

10. Drag the transition that you want to use between two clips in the timeline. Once the transition is added, it should appear in the timeline almost as a puzzle piece that links together the two clips.

11. Preview the sequence in your timeline by clicking in an empty area of the timeline (or in a gray area, like that above the timeline) to clear any individual clips, and press the Play button to watch the video you have created.

Using Editing Techniques and Styles

Now that you've had a chance to get familiar with editing clips in a timeline, it's important to consider how you will assemble these clips to create an interesting video. There are as many approaches to editing as there are people. However, there are principles that are applicable to the art of editing that you should know about, even if you decide (perhaps unwisely) not to use them. These principles and techniques have been proven to work and can be applied to a wide variety of projects with great success. In this section, we discuss only a few of the most popular techniques to use (or not use) while editing.

Before you make any editing decisions, consider the reasons for making a particular edit. Editing can be a process of experimentation, but you should know why you are doing something and have a good reason for it. More often than not, your editing decisions will be based on movement, rhythm, or for thematic reasons, although the "feel" of a cut is important in every instance. It can take awhile to develop a proper feel for editing, which is why it is important to practice often. In fact, you might try creating YouTube videos specifically as exercises to practice cutting scenarios, like a dialogue scene, a chase sequence, or some other short scenario (brushing your teeth, opening a door, etc.) just for the experience. Music videos also offer the opportunity to practice cutting on or off the beat.

In the process, you will learn quite a bit about shooting for editing as well. After all, if you don't have the footage that you need, such as the proper camera angles or shot types, then you won't have anything to edit. Check out other YouTube videos that you'd like to emulate and study their editing patterns. In a typical dialogue scene, for example, you might open with a wide or long shot of both actors, cut to a medium shot of your first actor, and then cut to a medium shot of the second actor, followed by a series of close-ups. In that scenario, the camera was shown to move in closer, becoming more intimate as we get familiar with the characters that are talking. At the same time, we are careful to maintain proper screen direction (as mentioned in Chapter 3) and pay attention to the actors' eyelines. The eyeline is where the actor is looking, and he should match up with the other actor he is looking at. Also, it's important to choose shots with the best framing, avoiding shots with too much headroom, or other potential mistakes made while shooting. Unfortunately, editing is not only assembling the ideal sequence, but also making the best out of the sometimes less-than-ideal footage you might be working with. It's up to you to decide what makes a scene interesting and highlight that with your editing, choosing the best shots and putting them in the right order to draw the viewer's attention where you want it to go and to make a compelling story.

Match Cutting

Match cutting is a technique that seamlessly links the action from one shot to the next (see Figure 3-7). Put another way, using a match cut allows you to create the illusion that an action continues from one shot to the next, such as someone picking up a glass in the first shot and continuing to lift and drink from it in the second. The main advantage to using a match cut is to make the viewer forget about the editing and focus on the action. Match cuts are unobtrusive, not because they are necessarily "invisible," but because they do not disrupt the flow of action (the opposite of a jump cut). This is not only useful for action films, where continuity of action is imperative, but also in documentaries or dramas. Shots may also be linked thematically, such as cutting from someone closing a door in one location and someone else opening it in another (or the same actor opening it in a completely different setting). There are different ways to use match cutting, but most often, it is simply used to make invisible cuts that link actions, particularly when moving from one shot type to another in the same scene. As another example,

FIGURE 3-7   A match cut between two shots creates a seamless flow of action.

a match cut is used when editing together the close-up shot of a hand picking up a phone, followed by the medium shot of the actor bringing it up to his or her ear. In this way, you can combine a variety of shot types as well.

Jump Cuts

Jump cuts are created when the middle portion of a clip is removed or when two clips are cut together whose angles are too similar or not dissimilar enough (see Figure 3-8). A jump cut produces a startling effect, the result of a break in continuity. Jump cuts can occur in a number of ways. One example would be cutting together an interview, shot from a single camera perhaps, and simply removing the space between questions, resulting in an interviewee's body that appears to suddenly jump or shift suddenly at the moment of the cut. One moment her body is a few inches or feet in one direction, and the next she is on the other side of the screen. The jump cut can be more or less obvious, depending on how much the subject shifts, but it is most often distracting. In any case, it is usually considered incorrect. Another example of a jump cut would be showing someone reaching for a glass in the first shot and then drinking from the glass in the second shot, with all of the matching action in between cut out. However, that doesn't mean a jump cut can't be useful. Godard famously used jump cuts in some of his films, and documentaries tend to do it when they need to move the action along quickly and cut down a long sequence, such as following a subject that is walking down a street. By removing portions in between clips, the action seems kind of jerky, but in a stylistic manner that viewers of reality TV are perhaps more comfortable with. You'll see this type of cut used on YouTube quite often, sometimes for comedic effect (such as in film or television parodies), as a stylistic choice, or as a way to cut out the unnecessary bits recorded during a diary entry or video podcast.

FIGURE 3-8   A jump cut is an often-jarring transition between two similar shots.

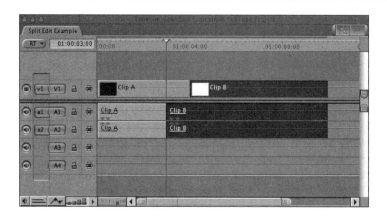

Split edits (also called "L" or "J" cuts) are often used with interviews and dialogue scenes.

Split Edits

A split edit, which is also known as an "L cut" or a "J cut," depending on how it's used (a reference to the physical shape or arrangement of clips in a timeline) refers to the transition between two shots when the audio cut does not occur at the same time as the video (see Figure 3-9). For example, when cutting a dialogue scene, you may hear subject B talking while we are looking at subject A (or at some other miscellaneous footage), followed by a visual cut a few seconds later to the person who was talking in the first shot. The audio from the second shot was used even though we weren't shown the corresponding video for that shot yet. This is done a lot in professional productions as a way to smooth over the cut from one shot to the next. In essence, the audio is leading the video, carrying us gently into the transition between clips. This cut can occur with audio that is heard before a shot is shown or when we are leaving a shot and its audio is still heard underneath the shot that follows. Whatever kind of video you are editing together, particularly if it involves dialogue of any kind, consider using a split edit as a way to smooth things out.

Applying Transitions and Special Effects

Transitions and special effects can be used to enhance your video by smoothing over cuts (in the case of transitions) or by matching colors and creating unusual looks with special effects. Within the realm of digital editing and effects, the number of options that are available to you are virtually limitless. Most editing software includes the basics, and even a bit more, for creating the results that you might expect from any other television show or even a film (see Figure 3-10).

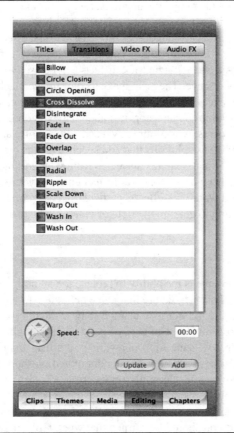

FIGURE 3-10   Applications like iMovie have a variety of possible transitions, although a simple dissolve or fade is usually best.

When applying transitions, make sure to use them sparingly. Overuse of transitions can make your video look cheap or unprofessional, particularly if you are using fancy transitions, like shape wipes. In fact, they can get downright annoying (add this one to the same category as zooming in and out too much while shooting video). Still, with tasteful application, cross dissolves and fades can be used quite a bit before they become tiresome. Of course, there is nothing wrong with straight cutting, without transitions. In most instances, that is actually preferred. Opening a movie with a fade in and closing it with a fade out is often appropriate. Using a dissolve or fade to imply the passage of time or the physical shift from one location to another is also fitting. Before adding a transition between your clips, consider how the transition is used and whether it adds something to your movie. Although they can sometimes smooth over imperfections in a cut, they should not be used as a panacea for poor editing.

Special effects fall under a wide range of categories, ranging from color correction (the most widely used on just about any video project) to stylistic effects, blurs, and distortions, not to mention advanced particle effects and 3-D graphics. For casual users, effects represent the flashy elements applied to a video, like "fairy dust" and "lens flare." However, effects can be much more than what is sometimes seen as a cheap magic trick. Effects can be used to subtly change the brightness, color, or contrast of a scene. They can make a color image black and white to simulate an old movie or flashback sequence, blur out portions of the screen to create an artificial depth-of-field effect or to smooth out wrinkles on an actor. Just about any video-editing software that you use comes with a selection of effects, while more advanced editing software offers a wider range of options, including the ability to use plug-ins that add specific features that were lacking in the host software. You may also choose to export your video from your editing software and import it into an application like After Effects or Motion to further enhance your video before outputting it. Learning how to animate and work with effects, particularly color correction, is highly recommended for anyone looking to get into the field of video production today.

Using AudioSwap

A relatively new feature of YouTube is the ability to replace the audio tracks on your videos with officially licensed music. This is a feature that came about due to ongoing problems with copyright infringement on the site. Rather than using a song without an artist's permission, which would ordinarily require some form of payment and legal wrangling, you can use one of the songs that YouTube has already licensed from a variety of artists and record labels. As part of the deal, you get to use the songs without worrying about getting sued, and the artists get to have their songs heard by more people. Currently (in its present TestTube configuration), most of the songs are from little-known musicians who can use the exposure. So if you'd like to use a song for your video's soundtrack, check out the music that is available through the AudioSwap feature on YouTube. However, you should be warned that when replacing your audio with one of these songs, your original audio will be permanently deleted. If this is your first time using the AudioSwap feature, try uploading a video to experiment with before potentially damaging a more important video.

NOTE *Always keep a backup of the original video and audio files that you edit in case you need to restore your original media.*

The following steps demonstrate how to replace the audio on one of your already uploaded videos with music licensed by YouTube. Of course, in order to accomplish this task, you must first have uploaded your video to your account on the YouTube Web site. If you are not already familiar with uploading videos, check out Chapter 4 for more information.

1. Click the TestTube link, located at the bottom of most YouTube pages, or go directly to the page by typing **www.youtube.com/testtube** in your browser's address bar.

2. Under the AudioSwap feature, which is currently listed on the TestTube area of the site, click Try It Out or click AudioSwap name.

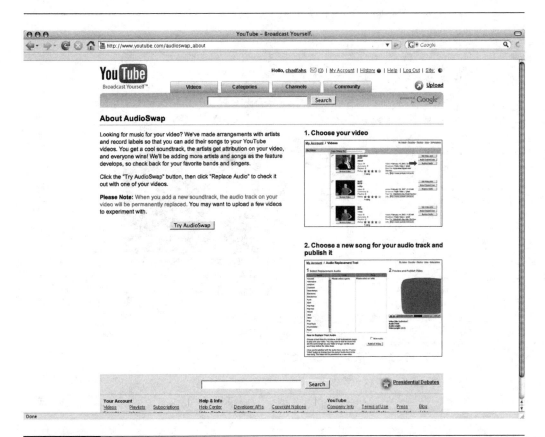

The AudioSwap feature allows you to replace your audio with music from an officially licensed song.

3. On the About AudioSwap page that appears, click the Try AudioSwap button (see Figure 3-11). If you haven't already logged on to your account, you will be asked to do so before proceeding to the next step. Simply enter your user name and password into the Member Login area of the page that appears, and click Log In. After logging on, the My Videos portion of your account page appears.

4. Decide which video you want to use the AudioSwap feature with, and click the Replace Audio button for that video. Once the AudioSwap page appears for your video, you should see an area on the left side of the page listing all of the song choices available to you (the section is labeled "Select Replacement Audio") and a preview of your chosen video file on the right (labeled "Preview And Publish Video").

5. Under Select Replacement Audio, click the Genre of music that you are most interested in using for your video, and then click the name of an Artist in the next column, as well as a particular song in the Track column (see Figure 3-12). Notice that information about

FIGURE 3-12 Select the type of music you want to apply to your video on the AudioSwap page.

the song appears in the Track column as well, such as the album name that it's from (if any), the length of the song, and any label it may be associated with. As soon as you select a track, your video plays back in the YouTube player on the right, providing you with a preview of your video combined with that particular song. If you don't like the current selection, or if the song is too long or too short for your video (the audio length and video length parameters under the player indicate this as well), simply choose a different track, different artist, or different genre altogether. Take your time to find a track that you like.

6. When you are done making your audio selection, click the Publish Video button to complete the AudioSwap feature. When a pop-up window opens that asks if you're sure you wish to change your audio track, simply click OK. At this point, you should be instantly returned to the My Videos portion of your account, with a note that indicates that your request is being processed. Next to your video's name, you should also see a note telling you that the audio swap is in progress, which can take a while to finish.

Working with Remixer

One of the latest and more interesting features added to YouTube is called Remixer. With this feature, you can edit together videos that are already uploaded to your account, add transitions between videos, and apply titles and effects, all without leaving YouTube. In addition, you can incorporate photos and music into the new video piece that you create. This is a particularly useful feature for videos that were uploaded directly to YouTube using the mobile upload or QuickCapture feature, since those videos were never passed through video-editing software of any kind. Now, with Remixer, you can make those videos a little more elaborate.

Editing your video online through a Web browser, without needing software on your computer, is an interesting idea that you're likely to see more of in the future. In fact, Remixer is not an original YouTube idea. It is based on software created by Adobe (it's really a rebranded "engine" derived from Adobe Premier Express). Presently, Remixer (like AudioSwap) is a feature of the TestTube area of the YouTube Web site.

One of the drawbacks to using Remixer is that you are limited to editing together the full video clips you have already uploaded, which means that you need to first upload your videos to YouTube before you can use Remixer. Although you are currently able to split clips into smaller parts and trim them as you would in most video editors, you are limited in how you can manipulate these clips, as compared with a full-featured editing application. Still, Remixer has its uses, and it wouldn't be surprising if more features are added when (or if) the feature catches on with the YouTube community.

Adding Clips to the Timeline in Remixer

The following steps describe how you can use Remixer to edit together clips. As of this writing, certain features were limited or disabled in the application, such as the use of music and photos, although those features (and others) will likely appear by the time you read this. There is also a built-in Help menu, located in the upper-right corner of the Remixer interface, which has a table of contents and a QuickStart tutorial to get you acclimated to using Remixer.

1. Click the TestTube link, located at the bottom of most YouTube pages, or go directly to the page by typing **www.youtube.com/testtube** in your browser's address bar.

2. Under the Remixer feature, which is currently listed on the TestTube area of the site, click Try It Out. If you haven't already logged on to your account, you will be asked to do so before proceeding to the next step. Simply enter your user name and password in the Member Login area of the page that appears, and click Log In. After logging on, the About YouTube Remixer – Engine by Adobe Premiere Express page appears.

3. On this page, click the Try Remixer button to launch the feature (see Figure 3-13). The Remixer interface appears, with a preview window on the left, a timeline underneath, and a video browser on the right.

YouTube's Remixer allows you to edit your uploaded video without leaving the site.

NOTE *In addition to immediately launching the Remixer interface, clicking the Try Remixer button activates this new feature for your account, which means that you can also access Remixer in the future by going to My Account, selecting My Videos, and then clicking the Remix Video button for a particular video.*

4. Once the Remixer interface appears and you have familiarized yourself a bit with its layout, make sure that all of your available videos are visible by clicking the My Videos link on the right side of the interface (this should already be visible by default). You should see a thumbnail and name for each video clip that has been uploaded to your account (see Figure 3-14). At this point, it's questionable whether videos that were encoded to the FLV (Flash Video) format prior to uploading will be included in the available videos listed here.

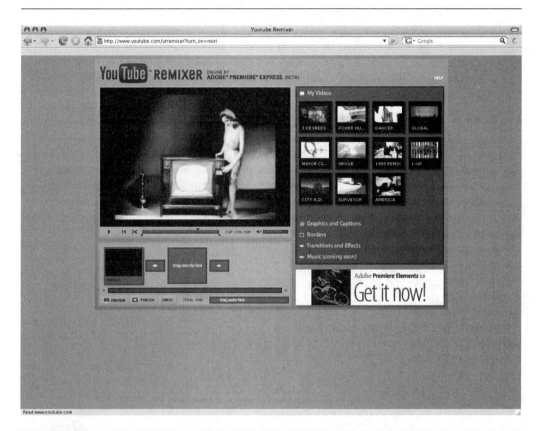

The Remixer interface offers many of the tools you might expect from ordinary video-editing software.

5. Drag one of the clips from the browser on the right to the left side of the timeline, where the Drag First Clip Here box is located.

6. Click the Play The Selected Clip button at the bottom of the viewer window to watch the individual clip play back. This step is optional if you already know what your clip looks like and are satisfied with its position in the sequence you are building. Notice that the running time for your clip is listed underneath the timeline (shown as Total) and below the viewer window. In addition, by pointing your mouse at individual clips in the timeline, you can see the total scene length (in Remixer, individual clips are referred to as "scenes").

7. If you wish to trim the length of a clip, drag the in and out points, located in the duration bar under the viewer window (represented by triangles that are currently located at the beginning and end of the clip's duration) until they rest on the new start and end frames that you want to use for the selected clip. Only the portion of the clip that falls within these points will be kept—everything that falls outside of these points will not be included. For example, you might want to combine clips that have extra black frames at the beginning and end of the clip, or clips that contain only a portion in the center that you want to use. By trimming your clips, you have much more control over what appears in your finished piece.

8. Drag another clip that you want to add to your sequence to the Drag Next Clip Here box, which is located immediately after your first clip. Now you are building a sequence of clips. Notice that the currently selected clip is highlighted red, while unselected clips are white.

9. Continue to add clips to the timeline, as covered in steps 5 through 7. As your sequence grows, you can navigate the timeline by dragging the scrollbar at the bottom back and forth or by clicking the arrow keys on either side of the scrollbar in order to see clips further down the timeline in any direction.

10. Click the Preview button at the bottom of the interface to watch your sequence thus far. A new viewer window opens on top of your screen, which shows your entire sequence as a finished movie. At this point, you may be satisfied with your new video piece, or you may wish to enhance it further by adding transitions between clips, creating a title or captions with some text, or applying graphics and special effects.

Adding Text and Graphics to a Video in Remixer

The following steps describe how you can use Remixer to apply text or graphics. Currently, it is only possible to add a single text or graphic element per clip, which means that you cannot overlay a title or captions as well as a graphic (such as glasses or a hat) on the same clip.

1. On the right side of the interface, click the Graphics And Captions link. A new portion of the browser appears, with a few options for captions and images that you might want to add to a particular video clip. You can scroll down in the browser to view all of the options that are currently available.

2. Click a clip in the timeline to select it (selected clips have a red highlight applied to them). In the next step, you will split this clip in order to add titles to a small portion at the beginning of the clip, rather than applying the text to the entire thing.

3. Drag the playhead for this clip (the downward-pointing triangle, which can be found in the bar directly below the viewer window) to a point where you want a title's text to end. For example, you might split the clip ten seconds after the start of the video. The current location of the playhead in your clip is listed on the left, and you can see the current frame in the viewer window.

4. Click the Scissors icon, located to the right of the clip's duration bar, to split the clip at this point. Your original clip is now separated into two separate clips. Now you can apply text or a graphic to the first, shorter clip without having to see that text appear over the entire clip.

5. With the first clip selected, drag a caption style from the browser on the right to the viewer window on the left. Again, it should be noted that text applied to a video clip stays on-screen for the duration of the selected clip. If desired, you can drag a graphic instead of text from the browser on the right to the viewer window on the left. At this time, you must choose between text or a graphic—you can't have both on the same clip.

6. Drag inside the text box that appears to highlight the text "click to edit," and then type a new title.

7. Select a font type from the drop-down menu that appears under your text in the viewer window. You can also click the color swatch to the right of the drop-down menu to select a color other than white for your text.

8. Drag the red outline surrounding your text or graphic to make it larger or smaller, scaling it to the precise size that you want it to be, and then drag inside the center of the text box to move it to the area of the screen where you want it to appear (top, center, bottom, left, or right).

Applying Transitions and Effects in Remixer

The following steps describe how to apply transitions between clips in Remixer. Currently, transitions are the only options available, although the category name in the browser (Transitions And Effects) implies that other effects will be added at some point.

1. On the right side of the interface, click the Transitions And Effects link. Once again, a new portion of the browser appears, with a few options for transitions and effects that you might want to add on or between video clips in the timeline.

2. Drag a transition, such as Fade To Black, from the browser on the right to the small box with arrows between two clips in the timeline. Transitions smooth the cut between two clips, usually by fading out and then fading back in to reveal the next clip in your sequence.

3. Click the Preview button at the bottom of the interface to watch your sequence thus far. As before, a new viewer window opens on top of your screen, which shows your entire sequence as a finished movie, including any transitions that you have applied.

4. At this point, if you are satisfied with your video, you can choose to publish it to YouTube by clicking the Publish button at the bottom of the YouTube Remixer interface.

Chapter 4

Uploading and Sharing Your Videos

How to...

- Optimize videos to look good on YouTube
- Determine important factors that affect video quality
- Examine YouTube-recommended settings
- Select an appropriate video codec for YouTube
- Upload videos to YouTube using video files, a webcam, and a mobile phone

Now that you've shot and edited some videos, it's time to upload those videos and share them with the world. This chapter covers all of the steps necessary to prepare your videos for uploading to the YouTube Web site, along with basic information about identifying your videos so that viewers can easily find them when conducting searches. The first section broadly covers issues that may affect image quality, followed by sections on manually encoding video prior to uploading, including more advanced operations that are important for experienced producers or adventurous amateurs. If you want to proceed directly to uploading videos, you can skip over the first sections on optimizing your video for YouTube. However, it is recommended for all users to familiarize themselves with the topics discussed here, since anyone may pick up a few tips for achieving better-looking video.

Optimizing Video for YouTube

Whenever you upload a video file to the YouTube Web site, it is converted into the FLV (Flash Video) and H.264 formats utilized by the site (H.264 is a recent addition to YouTube and is used for special devices like the iPhone, iPod, and AppleTV). As mentioned in the Introduction to this book, it is the FLV format, in particular, that makes it possible to deliver video to the widest range of users while offering special features, like the ability to easily embed and resize the video on a Web page. This also means that the video you upload is not the video that you'll see online. There is an intermediate step, at which point YouTube recompresses and "transcodes" the video (converts the video into a different format from the original) before you see it appear on the site. It's this process that significantly reduces the file size and image quality of your video. Unfortunately, you cannot observe or modify the transcoding process that YouTube uses. As soon as your video is uploaded, it is added to a queue, where it waits for its transformation to begin.

NOTE *Unless your video originates as an FLV file, it will be automatically compressed a second time when you upload it to YouTube and transcoded into the FLV format. The recommended settings that YouTube lists are simply intended to reduce the file size of your video so that you can upload it more easily, based on the bandwidth restrictions and file size limitations imposed by the Web site.*

If you look in the YouTube Help Center for information on uploading videos, you may notice that YouTube makes some general recommendations about how to optimize your videos for uploading to their site. The specifications that they list are fairly simple and will generally work for most users. However, these specifications are intended to be as broad and accessible as possible, focusing more on the balance between file size and image quality. Inevitably, image quality suffers. In this section, we discuss the YouTube-recommended formats, while also providing alternative solutions to get the best quality out of your video using more advanced methods. Considering the number of possible video formats that are being used by YouTube members to capture and output their videos, the focus here is on broader concerns, while delving into more detail on a few of the more common capture formats, such as DV (the DV format is associated with many tape formats and brand-specific marketing terms, such as MiniDV, DVCAM, Digital 8, and DVCPRO), as well as output formats such as MPEG-4.

Analyzing Your Video Prior to Uploading

The first point to consider prior to uploading your videos is the type and quality of your source material. For example, are you uploading low-quality cell phone and webcam images, such as video diaries, or are you interested in showcasing professional work that originated on DV, HDV, or even film? In a large part, it's a case of garbage in, garbage out. You always want to begin with the best-quality source material if you want to end up with good-looking video on YouTube. In some cases, such as vlogs (video blogs), this won't be a real concern. It's the nature of these videos to be "low-fi." Not to mention, many users of YouTube shoot their videos off-the-cuff or without any particular attention to format choices or image quality. After all, too much planning can spoil the fun (although it can be nice to surprise viewers by increasing the "production values" somewhat).

On the other hand, independent filmmakers and professional producers will want their video to look as close to the original source material as possible. Viewers expect narrative works, music videos, and movie trailers to look fairly crisp and clear. In fact, it can significantly detract from the enjoyment of a video when you can't discern important details in the image (see Figure 4-1). With regard to the quality of your source material, if the camera and video codec used to create the video were carefully chosen, then you're halfway there. The other half of the equation is using proper lighting and staging techniques to their maximum effect. As discussed in Chapter 2, there are many things that you can do while creating the video that will help to improve its quality, in particular, when it comes to videos that you upload and watch online. For example, videos without unnecessary details or visual complexities will fare better when transcoded to the FLV format (especially at the low data rates favored by YouTube).

In addition to the content and quality of your source material, the settings that you use to encode your video before uploading it have a significant effect on the final image quality. In most instances, the video that you produce with your camera is too large, both dimensionally and in file size, to be uploaded to the YouTube Web site. Although upload and download speeds, as well as server storage capacities, have improved dramatically in the past few years (due to declining costs of memory and the ubiquity of DSL, cable, and other high-speed network connections), we have a distance to go before uncompressed video and other large files can be moved freely about the Internet, much less delivered and stored inexpensively by a Web site that receives millions of users each day. This is why YouTube recommends encoding your video

FIGURE 4-1 One easily discernable difference between good video quality and bad video quality on YouTube can be seen when comparing "blocky" video with smooth video.

using a conservative set of criteria before uploading to its Web site. The results that you get from using the settings recommended by YouTube vary widely. Just take a look at the site itself for some examples. Is there a reason why the movie trailers and videos uploaded by film studios, record labels, and popular YouTube series (generally) look better than the heavily pixilated videos uploaded by casual users?

Once again, the reason for this difference in quality is twofold: The user is starting with relatively high-quality source material (as discussed, the video was shot well and used a video format with little or no compression), and the settings used to encode the video prior to uploading to YouTube were judiciously and carefully applied, using proper image proportions and optimum settings (or, alternately, doing the FLV compression before uploading to YouTube).

Consider, for example, a video shot using the popular DV format. Whether it was shot with a professional camera or with a small Sony Handycam, when it comes time to upload the video, some important choices must be made. First, how do we ensure that what we will see on YouTube accurately represents our source material as much as possible? A 1-minute piece of raw DV video (NTSC video standard) has a file size of approximately 228 megabytes (MB). Unfortunately, YouTube currently has a limit of 100 MB per file. Unless you are planning to keep your video segments to about 26 seconds, you'll need to recompress and transcode this video to another format before you can upload it to YouTube, where the process begins all over again. As a point of reference, the DV format applies 5:1 compression to the video that it captures, which means that, when compared to uncompressed, standard-definition video formats, you can fit five times as much DV information into the space required for uncompressed video. Now what if you had a 5-minute video that originated on the DV format and you wanted to upload it to YouTube? In order to meet the site's upload requirements, you would need to compress that 1.14-gigabyte (GB) file to under 100 MB using a wide variety of possible video codecs, resulting in a compression ratio of about 12:1—a significant reduction in file size. At the same time, you need to remember that YouTube will take that 100-MB file and reduce it even further, creating a file that is about 10 MB in size. At the end of the entire process, your original 1.14-GB DV file is reduced to a file that is approximately 10 MB in size—a compression ratio of 114:1. That's an extreme amount of compression! As another comparison, a DVD video created from the same DV source material uses a compression ratio of approximately 6:1. Apart from the very few lossless compression formats available, which typically use a 2:1 compression ratio—useless for Web video, compression is always done at the expense of image quality. Of course, any video formats for the Web must also account for audio as well, which takes up space and needs to be compressed with an equally complex array of codecs.

To summarize, what does this mean for the video that you upload to YouTube? Start with the best quality video that you can, and then make your compression decisions carefully before you upload. Unfortunately, some form of extreme compression is almost always required. If you decide to let YouTube handle your compression decisions, give it the best video that you can within its maximum file limitations. On the other hand, if you have the resources to create your own FLV files (as outlined in a later section of this chapter, titled "Achieving Better Results with Advanced Video Settings"), then you have total control over the final results. As you'll discover, this is not an option for everyone and can (more recently) produce unexpected results, but for those who have the time to experiment, it may be the best option for the highest quality results.

YouTube-Recommended Video and Audio Settings

The majority of YouTube members will allow YouTube to convert their videos for them, since it is often the simplest, most painless method to get your video on the site. It also eliminates the need for special software and other complicated processes. In this case, before we take a look at more advanced settings for videos that you upload to YouTube, we'll examine the standard settings recommended on the YouTube Web site.

The following video format and settings are recommended by YouTube:

- MPEG-4 (DivX, Xvid) format or other QuickTime, .mov, Windows .avi or .mpeg files
- 320 × 240 resolution
- MP3 audio
- Maximum file size: 100 MB
- Maximum length: 10 minutes

NOTE   *YouTube members with older Director accounts may be able to upload longer videos, since their accounts have been grandfathered in before the maximum time limit rules were changed.*

MPEG-4 and H.264

MPEG-4 and its variants can be found in use all over, not only on the Web (see Figure 4-2). For example, versions of MPEG-4 are used to create videos for Apple's iPod and iPhone, Sony's PlayStation Portable (PSP), and (optionally) for high-definition video content on Blu-ray and high definition (HD) DVD discs. MPEG-4 is a highly efficient and scalable codec that uses extreme data compression schemes while maintaining excellent quality (especially at the higher data rates). H.264 is one variation of MPEG-4 (H.264 is defined as MPEG-4 Part 10 or AVC, Advanced Video Coding) and produces better results than the generic MPEG-4 codec, although at the expense of greater encoding times and more complex, processor-intensive decoding. QuickTime 7 is one framework that supports H.264. Most video-editing applications, even those created for consumers, include an MPEG-4 export option. In theory, H.264 is a better choice for uploading to YouTube. You generally get twice the quality at the same file sizes as the standard MPEG-4 option. However, be careful when using any advanced codecs to upload to YouTube, since they might yield some unpredictable results, including "bad" frames and compression errors, which may appear randomly (often at the beginning of a clip) as a gray screen or otherwise blocky display. As a rule, make sure to test all of the videos that you upload. When it works, this codec works very well. In fact, it has been adopted for use with YouTube content that is delivered to iPhones, iPod, and AppleTV. Look for more information about H.264 to surface in the near future.

DivX and Xvid

The DivX codec is another lossy compression format that is commonly used in software that's designed to extract the contents of a DVD movie and reduce its file size for playback and storage on a computer or another video device. Technically speaking, it is also a variant of MPEG-4 (MPEG-4 Part 2 or MPEG-4 ASP) and can be created with a variety of resolutions and frame rates, although it is ideally suited for video content at 30 frames per second (NTSC video standard) and 25 frames per second (PAL video standard).

You can download the DivX player and converter for free from the DivX Web site (www .divx.com), and an inexpensive converter application is also available if you want higher-quality videos in this format (see Figure 4-3). DivX also hosts their own video content site, called

FIGURE 4-2 A wide variety of video devices use variations of the MPEG-4 standard.

FIGURE 4-3 You can download the DivX player and converter for free from the DivX Web site, although a DivX Converter application is for sale (with a short trial period).

Stage6, where users can "watch, share, and discuss DivX videos with friends." Sounds a lot like YouTube, right? The exception is that YouTube doesn't require a nonstandard video player to be installed like DivX does. Still, it's a useful format and worth checking into. As an added benefit, many DVD players will play back discs with DivX content on them (check the DVD player for the DivX-certified logo). Xvid is yet another variation on MPEG-4, although one that is open-source and not proprietary like DivX. It is also an extremely efficient codec, producing decent quality, even at compression ratios of 200:1 when compared to uncompressed video. You can visit www.xvid.org for more information about this particular codec.

Selecting a Video Codec for YouTube

If you dig a little deeper into the Help Center on YouTube's Web site, you'll notice that they also generally recommend that you save your videos as either QuickTime, .mov, Windows .avi or .mpeg files before attempting to upload them. Their specific recommendations are still MPEG4 format (DivX, Xvid) at 320×240 resolution with MP3 audio. However, it does indicate that you can upload certain QuickTime and Windows Media file formats, without specifying what those are.

For Mac users, virtually every video format, whether it's DV, MPEG2, or H.264, is delivered in a QuickTime container (a "wrapper" for video). When you see the .mov extension on a file, you know that it will most likely be readable by the QuickTime Player installed on a Mac, or even through the free QuickTime Player available for computers running Windows. Even without the .mov file extension, you should see the QuickTime icon associated with video-related file extensions. For example, .mp4 is a common MPEG-4 file extension and will play back using QuickTime. On a PC, you may see Windows .avi files instead of QuickTime's .mov extension, although both may be encountered, depending on the software you have installed. Ultimately, it's quite likely that if you can play the video file on your computer, YouTube can accept it as long as it meets the requirements for file size and length.

Of course, other complicating factors can affect universal playback of a file, like the specific codec used to create the video and the version of the player software that generated the original file (for example, QuickTime 7 files may not play properly using QuickTime 6). Still, file extensions like .mov are a pretty good indicator of what works and what doesn't. The trouble, as mentioned, arises when working with files that were created using new formats, with special settings and proprietary codecs that do not have support across all computers or Web browsers. Even FLV files created specifically for YouTube or other video sites will differ, and you may encounter difficulties if trying to upload them to YouTube without making sure that they match the rather hazy requirements. Also, recent updates to the YouTube Web site have made it potentially more difficult to work with FLV files that are uploaded by users, although this may change with future updates.

So what are some basic codec choices and settings that you can use to prepare your video for uploading to YouTube? Following this paragraph is a list of a few high-quality formats that may prove useful for videos that you upload to the site. These options should provide a decent (though not always appropriate) balance of file size versus quality. Of course, some tweaking and testing may be required. Also, depending on the computer platform you are working on (Mac or PC) and the software you are using to do the preparation (iMovie, Final Cut Pro, QuickTime Pro, Premiere, Windows Movie Maker, etc.), the actual names and options may vary. Ideally, you can get underneath the presets and view the specific codec that is being used to compress the video. For example, you might see a preset in your export options that says Broadband—High, LAN/Intranet, or a variety of similar preset names. If you are able to click the Options button (or equivalent), such as in QuickTime Pro, then you can see whether this preset is using MPEG-4, H.264, Sorenson Video 3, or some other codec. As mentioned, obtaining the best result is usually a process of trial and error. You can try one codec to compress your video and then compare it with another, nearly equivalent option. This is especially relevant if you are trying to squeeze a large video file (generally, anything more than a few minutes in length) to meet the stringent requirements for YouTube.

The following are several video formats that, at the appropriate data rates, may work well when uploading to YouTube while also maintaining adequate video quality:

- Photo-JPEG
- Sorenson Video 3
- MPEG-4
- H.264
- WMV
- DivX
- Xvid

Video-encoding software and hardware, including the proprietary processes employed by YouTube, analyze and transcode (convert one video format to another) incoming video according to a complex set of algorithms (mathematical processes and sets of rules), which look at things like how often a change occurs from one frame to the next and which kinds of data can be eliminated with the least sacrifice in quality (e.g., removing color information and selectively degrading resolution). It's an extremely tricky game to play, even for the most advanced encoders. Therefore, by providing YouTube with the best input, you help their encoders do a good job, which ensures the best output results.

Photo-JPEG   Out of the choices mentioned in the last section, Photo-JPEG is a good format for uploading to YouTube if you intend to have YouTube perform the conversion of video into FLV for you. Photo-JPEG is an intraframe, or all I frame, codec, which means that every frame is treated as a unique frame, like a sequence of photographs or film. This means that you won't encounter the odd motion artifacts that are prevalent in interframe formats like MPEG-2 and MPEG-4. Interframe formats, by comparison, look at a sequence of frames over time and only store the information that changes. This process works well to reduce the overall file size. However, Photo-JPEG produces much larger file sizes, but preserves more quality by including every frame, regardless of its contents. Be forewarned that your video gamma (color levels) may shift as a result of converting to Photo-JPEG, creating more saturated images.

When using Photo-JPEG compression, try using a quality setting of approximately 50, while going as high as 75 if your video is relatively short. The quality slider that is usually associated with the Photo-JPEG codec is primarily a way to tell the compressor how high the data rate should be. A higher number will produce better results, but larger file sizes. Eventually, you reach a point of diminishing return, where the file sizes keep climbing without seeing any visible improvements. You might need to experiment with quality settings, depending on the nature of your source material, the length of your video, and the file sizes that result. When encoding a DV video file that is approximately 1 minute and 30 seconds in length and 300 MB in size, a quality setting of 50 produces a 40-MB file, a setting of 75 produces a 70-MB file, and a setting of 100 yields a 250-MB file. As you can see, there is an exponential leap in file size between a setting of 75 ("High") and a setting of 100 ("Best"), with no perceptible difference in quality. In fact, at this point, it would have made more sense to use the original DV file—provided it was under the 100-MB limit—rather than choose a high quality setting for the Photo-JPEG codec.

WMV   If you're working on a PC and are using any of the applications that came with the Windows operating system (such as the Windows Movie Maker software), then you are most likely familiar with the WMV format. In fact, WMV files (Windows Media Video) are one of the most popular and ubiquitous formats on a PC. They produce relatively good quality output, and at high bit rates, such as 512 kbps (kilobits per second) or 1 Mbps (megabits per second), can be more than satisfactory for uploading video to YouTube. When you produce a movie with the Windows Movie Maker application, for example, your output options are somewhat limited, being restricted to a standard AVI-DV codec, as well as a variety of Web presets, which are all variations of the WMV format. Curiously, WMV is yet another format that has its roots within the MPEG-4 codec.

Additional Recommendations before Encoding Your Video

Before you proceed to finally uploading your videos to YouTube, consider a few additional steps that might help to improve the overall quality of your encoded videos. The first step, which is optional, is to deinterlace your video, followed by resizing your video to match the frame size utilized by YouTube, as well as reformatting any widescreen videos (16:9 aspect ratio) to play within a standard 4:3 frame.

Deinterlacing Your Video

Video that is shot using a standard video camera is most often interlaced, which means that each frame is divided into two separate "fields." NTSC video, which is used in countries like the United States and Japan, is comprised of 30 frames of video per second, or 60 fields per second. Fields may be either odd or even, with each field comprised of scan lines that are written using every other line in an image. Odd fields are written starting with scan lines 1, 3, 5, 7, etc. Even fields are written using lines 2, 4, 6, 8, etc. When combined, these fields make up a complete frame of video. The use of interlacing is only pertinent to playback on televisions, which (until the advent of digital TVs) are most often interlaced. On the other hand, computers use progressive scan displays, which means that entire frames are written at once and do not require separation into fields. As a result, video looks best on a computer when it originates as a progressive scan format or when interlaced video is deinterlaced to create a progressive scan image. If the software that you use to output movies for YouTube includes the ability to deinterlace your video, now is a good time to utilize that feature. This feature is often listed under filters or as an additional option (often a check box) in your chosen output module. Many of the Web presets in video-encoding software automatically deinterlace the video for you, since the assumption is that any video produced for the Web will be viewed on a computer monitor and not on a standard television.

Resizing Your Video

YouTube requires that all of its video be stored with an image size of 320×240 pixels (even though it scales it up to 425×350 for playback), and any video that you upload will be resized to these dimensions whether you like it or not (see Figure 4-4). Of course, it's likely that your video began at a size that is at least twice those dimensions (640×480, 720×480, or larger), in which case, you'll ensure the best results by doing the resizing yourself before uploading to YouTube. You'll also reduce the file size of the video that you upload by doing the resizing first, thereby saving extra data that can be used to increase the bit rates that you encode with, resulting in a vast improvement in quality. Most output options for editing software, encoders, or other video applications include the option to resize video manually or to apply a size change as part of an already created preset. Make sure to check the descriptions or information associated with a particular preset to make sure that the file size you end up with is 320×240 pixels and not a size that is larger or smaller.

Creating Letterbox for Widescreen Formats

With the universal acceptance of digital television standards—high-definition television (HDTV) in particular—video with 16:9 aspect ratios is becoming the norm. In fact, any high-definition format that you use is, by necessity, 16:9, since it is an integral part of the standard. Even standard-definition footage may originate and be displayed as 16:9 video if it employs anamorphic settings (16:9 video that is squeezed and stretched to fit into a 4:3 video file for storage and then stretched back out to fill a widescreen television). In either case, you may have video that is in a wider aspect ratio than can be correctly used by YouTube. In order to solve this

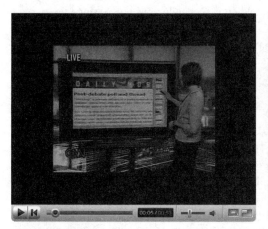
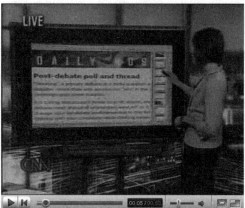

FIGURE 4-4   YouTube requires that your video dimensions be 320×240 pixels, which is a little less than the dimensions that YouTube will use to scale the embedded video up 425×350 for playback on a page.

FIGURE 4-5   For the best results, widescreen video that originated at a 16:9 aspect ratio
should be letterboxed in a 4:3 frame before uploading it to YouTube.

problem, you'll need to letterbox your 16:9 video inside a standard 4:3 video window, which results in the black bars on the top and bottom of the image (see Figure 4-5). These bars are often associated with a cinematic look, as seen when watching films on television. It's really just an operation to allow the full widescreen image to be viewed without cropping it. In fact, it's probably best to think of the black space at the top and bottom of the frame as what it basically is: empty, unused space. You'll even save some data when you encode your video, since the black space takes up very little bandwidth when it's encoded.

In the next few sections, you will learn how to prepare your video and encode it using some of the popular video applications on the market. The choice of applications by no means represents all of your options, but it should give you a good idea of the settings you might want to use with your own software.

Encoding Video for YouTube Using QuickTime Pro

Whether you're working on a Mac or a PC, QuickTime Pro is a simple and useful addition to your multimedia toolkit. While the standard QuickTime Player application is free to download from Apple's Web site and comes preinstalled on all Macs, updating to QuickTime Pro (which costs $29.99) adds the capability to export videos using a wide array of delivery formats. It also includes some other nice features, like the ability to save movies that you find online and to perform simple edit operations, like cutting, pasting, and trimming video clips. In addition, the QuickTime Pro export options and dialog boxes are seen (in some form) in just about every video export menu of software on a Mac, including applications like iMovie and Final Cut Pro.

The following steps illustrate one method to prepare your video for YouTube using QuickTime Pro:

1. Launch the QuickTime Pro application by double-clicking a QuickTime movie to open it, or by choosing File | Open File and using the Open window to locate a video on your hard drive.

2. With the movie open in a QuickTime window, choose File | Export.

3. In the Save As text field of the Save Exported File As dialog box, type a name for your movie file.

4. Using the Save Exported File As dialog box, choose a location on your hard drive where you want to save the new file you are about to create.

5. At the bottom of the dialog box, click the Export down arrow, and select Movie To QuickTime Movie. There are other default choices in this drop-down menu that may work equally well, including Movie To MPEG-4. For the best results with the most control, however, choose Movie To QuickTime Movie.

6. Click the Options button to the right of the Export drop-down menu. The Movie Settings window opens.

7. At the top of the Movie Settings dialog box, in the area labeled Video, click the Settings button (see Figure 4-6).

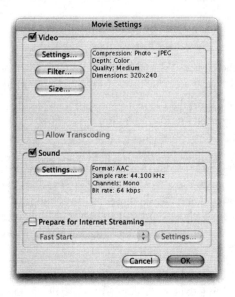

FIGURE 4-6   The Movie Settings dialog box in QuickTime Pro

8. At the top of the Standard Video Compression Settings window that opens, select Photo – JPEG from the Compression Type drop-down menu. At this point, you may choose from a variety of other QuickTime codecs as well, including Sorenson Video 3, H.264, or MPEG-4 Video, to name a few. The choice partially depends on the source material you are converting and how much of it you need to convert.

9. In the section labeled Compressor, drag the Quality slider to the Medium position (50 percent). Also, make sure that the Frame Rate field is set to Current. The Data Rate field is set to Automatic by default, and can be left there.

10. Click OK to accept the new settings in the Standard Video Compression Settings window.

11. Back in the Movie Settings window, click the Size button.

12. In the Export Size Settings window that opens, choose 320 × 240 QVGA from the Dimensions drop-down menu.

13. Make sure that the Deinterlace Source Video check box is selected. Also, if you have 16:9 source material, you may decide to select the Preserve Aspect Ratio Using check box and select the Letterbox option.

14. Click OK to accept the choices you made in the Export Size Settings window.

15. In the Movie Settings window, make sure that the Sound check box is selected, and click the Settings button.

16. Select AAC from the Format drop-down menu, select Mono from the Channels drop-down menu (YouTube will convert audio to mono), and select 44.100 from the Rate drop-down menu. Under the Render Settings area, choose Best from the Quality drop-down menu, with a Target Bit Rate setting of 64 Kbps or higher.

17. Click OK to accept the choices you made in the Sound Settings window, and click OK again to accept the choices you made in the Movie Settings window.

18. When you're ready to export the file using the settings you just made, click the Save button in the Save Exported File As dialog box.

Encoding Video for YouTube Using Windows Movie Maker

If you're working on a PC, you can use a wide variety of applications to export your movies for uploading to YouTube. The default application that most (if not all) PC users have access to is called Windows Movie Maker, which is somewhat similar to iMovie on a Mac. The following steps demonstrate how to use one of the presets in Windows Movie Maker to export your video for uploading to YouTube:

1. From the Start menu, choose All Programs | Windows Movie Maker to launch the application, or (if you've moved the location of the application or created a shortcut to it) find its application icon on your computer, and click it to begin.

2. Choose File | Import, and select a video from a location on your hard drive using the Import File window, or select one of the Import options (such as Videos) from the Task area on the left side of the interface.

3. When you've located a video that you want to import, click Import.

4. Drag a video clip (or multiple clips) to the timeline at the bottom of the screen. Depending on how your application is set up, you may need to toggle from the Storyboard view to the Timeline view.

5. Under the Publish To category in the Task options, choose This Computer, and then click Next to begin the export process.

6. From the Publish To dialog box that appears, make sure your video has a title, select My Computer or another location on your computer, and click Next.

7. In the Publish Movie dialog box that appears, select the desired output options for your movie, including quality and file size. In general, a 512-Kbps WMV file with a display size of 320×240 pixels at 30 frames per second is a fine setting for uploading to YouTube. Try to choose the best quality (highest bit rate) you can while still keeping the file size under the 100-MB limit for uploading to YouTube.

8. Click Publish to begin saving your movie, and then click Finish when you are done.

Achieving Better Results with Advanced Video Settings

Now that you've seen what YouTube recommends, as well as a couple of ways to produce videos that match its requirements, let's examine some alternative approaches to optimizing your video for upload to the YouTube Web site. If you are really interested in realizing the best quality possible on YouTube, then you need to consider converting your original source video directly to the FLV format, prior to uploading. This results in skipping a generation of compression, saving those extra steps discussed in the last section, which significantly degrades the quality of your video. By going directly to FLV, you control exactly how your video will look on YouTube— what you see is what you get. Not only does it (potentially) improve the results that you see, it also makes your videos easier to upload (much smaller file sizes) and eliminates the long waits that can occur while YouTube transcodes your video. However, you should be forewarned that recent changes to the YouTube Web site may limit the ability to properly use FLV files uploaded by users. This is partially due to users trying to exploit loopholes in the file size constraints by using the FLV format. At this time of this writing, users were beginning to experience difficulties with this format, although this may change over time (for better or worse).

NOTE   *If you're new to Web video, you can choose to skip this discussion. However, if you are not content with the results that you get by directly uploading the videos that are generated by your editing software, webcam, or other video-capturing device, then it may be useful to consider the alternatives that are available to you. However, with constant changes to the security and feature set of the YouTube Web site, it's becoming more difficult to know whether FLV files created by a user prior to uploading will work as expected.*

As the popularity of Flash Video continues to grow, thanks in large part to sites like YouTube, more software becomes available to produce FLV files. Still, at the time of this writing, inexpensive Flash Video encoders are hard to find. Commonly used professional FLV encoding solutions include Sorenson Squeeze (available for PC and Mac), On2 Flix (PC and Mac), and Flip4Mac Episode (Mac only). For the purposes of our discussion, we will talk primarily about Sorenson Squeeze, since it's a cross-platform and also happens to be an excellent choice for professionals and other demanding users.

NOTE *Sorenson Squeeze can be used for a wide variety of encoding tasks, including producing file formats for the Web, DVD, portable devices (even the PSP) and high-definition video discs.*

Encoding Video with Sorenson Squeeze

Sorenson Squeeze is an excellent choice for producing high-quality FLV files for YouTube. If you are an aspiring filmmaker or a professional producer, an application like Squeeze can take your YouTube videos to the next level of quality. You can find out more about Squeeze by visiting Sorenson's Web site at www.sorensonmedia.com.

NOTE *As an added benefit, Squeeze (and applications like it) comes with an FLV player, which allows you to easily preview the Flash Video files that you create. The FLV format is rather strange, in that it cannot be viewed without special players, which can be hard to come by if you don't have the Flash Video application. These files do not currently play back in QuickTime or Windows Media Player, so you'll need a player application to see the results produced by your favorite encoder. An example of a free FLV player includes the latest version of the VideoLAN (VLC) media player, available from www.videolan.org.*

The following steps demonstrate how to create an FLV file that you can upload to YouTube using Sorenson Squeeze:

1. Open Sorenson Squeeze by clicking its application icon in your Applications folder (Mac) or by using the Start menu (PC).

2. After Sorenson Squeeze launches, locate a file on your hard drive by opening a Finder window (Mac) or navigating to a folder that is clearly visible from the desktop (PC). The floating-window design of Sorenson Squeeze makes it easy to position or move the application window around the screen while having other windows open at the same time.

3. Drag a video file to the main Batch window, located at the bottom of the Sorenson interface. The video you drag appears under an assigned "job" in the Batch list and is displayed in the Preview window at the top of the interface (see Figure 4-7).

4. In the Format & Compression Settings area of the interface, located to the left of the Batch list, use the down arrow to the left of the Macromedia Flash Video (.flv) settings to reveal its contents (see Figure 4-8).

FIGURE 4-7   The Sorenson Squeeze application interface

5. Select a preset, such as 512K or VP6_512K (depending on what version of Sorenson you have), and drag it to the video file in the Batch list to the right. The preset should appear underneath the video that is below the first job.

TIP   *Although it is an FLV file, file sizes that are too large can be tedious to download, even though the quality may look excellent at high data rates. A quality of about 512 usually produces good results, which is about twice the size that you would get from allowing YouTube to do the transcoding for you. Once you approach 1 Mbps, the video takes a while to download, unless you're on a very fast connection. Still, if it's the highest quality that you are after, you might test out these settings and verify the results.*

FIGURE 4-8 Locate a Macromedia Flash Video (.flv) preset in the Format & Compressions Settings window.

6. When you are ready to export your video, click the Squeeze It! button in the lower-right corner of the application interface. The video is sent to the original location of your source file, appended with the name of the preset you chose and a unique number.

7. Once your video is finished encoding, locate the file on your hard drive, and drag it to the Sorenson FLV Player application icon (located in the same Applications folder as Squeeze) to preview your encoded video. The player makes it easy to preview FLV files, which require a special player to watch (see Figure 4-9).

FIGURE 4-9 Sorenson FLV Player allows you to preview the FLV files that you create.

TIP *You can apply as many presets as you want to the same video file in the Batch list and then render several different versions of your video with various quality settings. The benefit to doing this is that you can test file sizes and image quality to get the best balance of the two.*

NOTE *You can double-click a preset in the Format & Compression Settings window to see the specific settings that were used to create the preset you've chosen or are thinking about choosing. In the Audio/Video Compression Settings window that opens, you may also modify the preset to create your own custom settings. In general, the settings that have been created for you work well, and unless you're familiar with the different options that you see here, it's best to stick with the default presets. The one exception might be frame size, since you already know that YouTube requires pixel dimensions of 320 × 240.*

Working with Analog Video Formats

So far in our discussion, the assumption has been that your video originated in a digital format, such as the video created by a digital video camcorder, recorded on a mobile phone, or imported directly into your computer from a webcam or other device. For users of analog video formats (such as VHS, Hi8, and 8mm), uploading video is a more circuitous process. Digital video is defined by a string of 1s and 0s, which is the binary information utilized by computers and any other digital device to store data. Once data is in a digital format, it can be easily transmitted, copied, and used over and over again without any loss in quality. Analog video, on the other hand, is comprised of a physical waveform that is not so easy to pin down—at least, not without losing information along the way. When you want to upload video to YouTube that you shot on a Hi8 camera, for example, what options do you have? First, you need a device that can convert analog video signals to digital information. Companies like Canopus and ADS make relatively inexpensive devices for just this purpose (see Figure 4-10). Professionals might use an input device from companies like AJA or Blackmagic-Design. However, the least expensive

FIGURE 4-10   Video converter boxes, like those sold by Canopus, are useful for getting your analog video into a digital format that you can edit and upload to YouTube.

method for capturing and working with analog video may be another video camera (if you already have one), since some camcorders will allow you to pass analog video from composite or S-Video inputs to its FireWire output and into your computer. Alternately, you may (depending on your camera or digital video deck) record the analog video onto another digital tape. Then, after recording the video in a digital format like DV, transfer it to your computer using a wide variety of editing software, as discussed in Chapter 3.

TIP *How ever you decide to convert your analog video to a digital format, make sure to reduce the number of steps in the conversion process to as few as possible. Since you are already losing data when making the move from analog to digital (for example, from VHS to DV), make sure that you are working with the best source material available (the original master tape or closest to it). Also, despite the marketing hype, DVD-Video is not a good archival medium or satisfactory intermediate step for converting video that will be recompressed or edited. At this point in time, the DV format is one of the most practical and (for most purposes, particularly with regard to consumers or small studios) highest quality formats that you can record your analog material onto.*

Uploading Videos to Your YouTube Channel

Once you've prepared your videos for uploading to the YouTube Web site, you're ready to begin the final step in the process. In fact, the uploading process consists of two simple steps. The first step requires you to enter basic information to identify your video, while the second step involves selecting the file that you want to upload and choosing a privacy setting for it.

The following steps describe how to upload videos to your channel on the YouTube Web site:

1. Click the Upload button in the upper-right corner of the YouTube Web site. If you haven't already logged on, enter your user name and password into the Member Login area of the page that appears, and click Log In. After logging on, the Video Upload page appears.

2. In the Title text field, enter a unique name for your video. If possible, use a short title that is descriptive and clearly identifies the contents of your video (maximum of 60 characters). See Figure 4-11 for an example.

3. Type a brief explanation of your video in the Description text field.

4. In the Tags field, enter several keywords (each one separated by a space), which make your videos easier to find when other users are searching for them using matching criteria. In theory, these tags will also help to display your videos under groups of related videos on individual video pages. Tags are discussed in greater detail in Chapter 6.

5. Under the Video Category section, choose one category type to associate with your video by clicking the appropriate option. Categories make your videos easier to find for users who prefer to browse for videos according to content type. Choices include Autos & Vehicles, Comedy, Entertainment, Film & Animation, Gadgets & Games, Howto & DIY, Music, News & Politics, People & Blogs, Pets & Animals, Sports, and Travel & Places (see Figure 4-12).

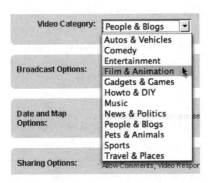

FIGURE 4-11   The first sections of the Video Upload page that you need to fill out include Title, Description, and Tags.

FIGURE 4-12   Select a category to help others who might browse YouTube find your video.

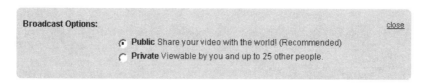

Choose whether you want to make the video accessible to the general public or just to yourself and those you specify.

6. Under the Broadcast Options area of the Video Upload page, click Choose Options, and then select either the Public or Private option, depending on the privacy setting you prefer for your video. As listed on the page, the options are Public: Share Your Video With The World! (Recommended) and Private: Only Viewable By You And Up To 25 Other People (see Figure 4-13). If you've created a contact list in your account (discussed in Chapter 5), you can complete the Date And Map Options and Sharing Options areas, although they are not required and are discussed in Chapter 7.

7. When you are finished entering the required information, click the Upload A Video button at the bottom of the Video Upload page. The Video Upload (Step 2 of 2) page appears.

8. Click the Browse button at the top of the page to select the video that you want to upload. Remember, your video is limited to a maximum file size of 100 MB and may be no longer than 10 minutes in length.

9. Navigate to the file on your computer that you want to upload using the File window that opens, and click Open to select the file.

10. When you are finished making the necessary settings on both Video Upload pages, click the Upload Video button at the bottom of the page. YouTube presents you with a page that shows the progress of your video upload. When the upload is complete, YouTube will present you with your video information, including a code to embed the video in a Web page.

According to YouTube, uploads take approximately 1 to 5 minutes per megabyte, depending on your connection speed. Estimated upload times assume that you are using a high-speed connection. In fact, it is difficult to determine how long an upload will take. At this point, you may choose to walk away from your computer and take a break, especially if you are uploading a large video file.

Capturing Video Directly to YouTube with Quick Capture

If you have a webcam connected to your computer, or if your computer has one built in (like Apple's MacBooks do, for example), then you can bypass the entire video creation and optimization process. Instead, Quick Capture allows you to record your video live, right from your webcam, directly to the YouTube Web site. Of course, this means that you cannot edit your video or otherwise manipulate it in many ways. Instead, what you get is instant gratification and a lot of time saved on editing videos where production value and picture quality are not of paramount concern. Typically, the videos that work best for Quick Capture are video diaries and vlogs which are usually spontaneous, improvised, and timely snapshots that do not require much forethought.

The following steps describe how to use the Quick Capture feature when uploading video to YouTube:

1. Make sure your webcam is installed and functioning properly.

2. Click the Upload button in the upper-right corner of the YouTube Web site. If you haven't already logged on, enter your user name and password into the Member Login area of the page that appears, and click Log In. After logging on, the Video Upload page appears.

3. In the Title text field, enter a unique name for your video. If possible, use a short title that is descriptive and that clearly identifies the contents of your video.

4. Type a brief explanation of your video in the Description text field.

5. In the Tags field, enter several keywords (each one separated by a space), which make your videos easier to find when other users are searching for them using matching criteria. In theory, these tags will also help to display your videos under related videos on individual video pages.

6. Under the Video Category section, choose one category type to associate with your video by clicking the appropriate option. Categories make your videos easier to find for users who prefer to browse according to content type. Choices include Autos & Vehicles, Comedy, Entertainment, Film & Animation, Gadgets & Games, Howto & DIY, Music, News & Politics, People & Blogs, Pets & Animals, Sports, and Travel & Places. In addition, you may complete the Broadcast Options, Date And Map Options, and Sharing Options areas before proceeding to the next step, although this is optional.

7. When you are finished entering the required information, click the Use Quick Capture button at the bottom of the Video Upload page.

8. In the area of the page labeled Video Upload – Quick Capture (Step 2 of 2), make sure that the appropriate device is selected from the Camera drop-down menu in the upper-left corner of the Preview window. You can also click the orange Auto-Detect Camera & Mic button that is in the center of the window (see Figure 4-14).

9. Make sure the appropriate audio input is selected from the Audio drop-down menu in the upper-right corner of the Preview window.

10. When you see a picture from your camera in the window, click the Record button to begin recording your video.

11. Click the Done button when you are finished recording. Alternately, you can click the Re-Record button if you'd like to start over. This is a good option when you are trying to get a monologue just right.

FIGURE 4-14   Make sure your video camera or webcam is connected, and click the Auto-Detect Camera & Mic button.

Uploading Video from a Mobile Phone

In addition to the typical upload options for files that originate on a computer, YouTube supports the direct upload of videos generated by a mobile phone or other portable device, such as a personal digital assistant (PDA), as shown in Figure 4-15. If your device can capture video and send Multimedia Messaging Service (MMS) messages, and you have an Internet service

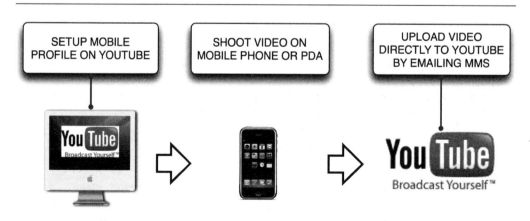

FIGURE 4-15   The workflow for YouTube's mobile upload option

or data plan with your mobile phone provider, then you can upload the videos you create, no matter where you are located. Imagine shooting a video on your phone while at the beach, on the train, or in the office, and then instantly sending it to your YouTube channel for everyone to see. Support for this feature depends on the service provider that you use for your mobile phone. Currently, this feature supports uploads from Cingular, Sprint, T-Mobile, and Verizon.

In order to upload videos from your mobile phone to YouTube, you first need to set up a mobile upload profile for your account. Once you've done this, YouTube will give you an e-mail address that is unique to your account where you can send your videos from your mobile device. Videos that you send to this address will be instantly uploaded to your channel, along with the settings that you defined in the mobile upload profile.

TIP *You can set up two mobile upload profiles if you intend to use more than one mobile device, such as a mobile phone and a PDA (or two different phones), or if you want to have multiple types of upload profiles with different default titles, descriptions, and tags.*

The following steps describe the process to create a new mobile upload profile:

1. Click the Upload button in the upper-right corner of the YouTube Web site. If you haven't already logged on, enter your user name and password into the Member Login area of the page that appears, and click Log In.

2. Click the Set Up Your Preferences button, located next to the mobile phone graphic on the right side of the page (see Figure 4-16). You may access the same option by logging onto your account and choosing Mobile Profile from the Account Settings area of the My Account page.

3. On the Mobile Profile page, click the Create Mobile Profile button (see Figure 4-17).

4. Enter a mobile phone number and mobile provider that will identify this particular profile (see Figure 4-18).

5. Enter a video title, which is applied by default to the beginning of every file you upload and is appended with either a file name or date.

TIP *You can override the default title for individual files by typing* **t:** *and then your desired title into the body of the e-mail that you send to your assigned e-mail address at YouTube.*

FIGURE 4-16   The Set Up Your Preferences button on the Video Upload page will take you directly to the Mobile Profile page.

FIGURE 4-17   Click the Create Mobile Profile button to create a new profile for your phone or other mobile, video-enabled device.

6. Select the Filename or Date check box to specific the information that will be added to the end of your video title, which makes it unique and easy to identify.

7. Add a description for your video, which is applied by default to every file that you upload.

8. Specify whether you want the videos that you upload to by public (available to anyone visiting the YouTube Web site) or private (only available to yourself and the friends you choose) by selecting the appropriate option.

9. Type any tags that you want to add to your videos by default, making sure to separate them with spaces, as usual. Typical tags include "mobile," "video," and "cellphone," but you can use any tags that you feel are appropriate or that will make your videos easier to find.

10. Select a suitable category from the Category drop-down menu, such as Travel & Places or People & Blogs.

11. If you want to automatically share videos that you upload from your mobile device with your friends, enter their e-mail addresses in the Share text box, separating the addresses with commas.

12. Under the Notification area, select or clear the check boxes that specify whether you want to be notified by e-mail or text message when your video is uploaded. Options include E-mail Me When Video Upload Is Complete and Reply Via Text Message When The Upload Is Complete.

13. When you're done filling in all of the necessary fields on this page, click the Save Profile button.

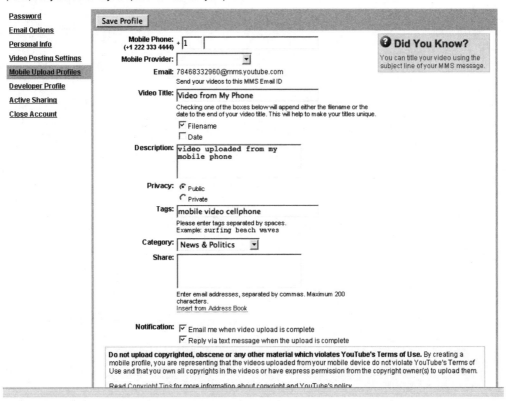

My Account / Mobile Profile

Mobile Upload lets you upload videos to YouTube directly from your mobile phone. Once you add your phone number and create your profile, it only takes a few keys to upload via MMS from your phone.

Password
Email Options
Personal Info
Video Posting Settings
Mobile Upload Profiles
Developer Profile
Active Sharing
Close Account

Save Profile

Mobile Phone: (+1 222 333 4444) +1
Mobile Provider:
Email: 78468332960@mms.youtube.com
Send your videos to this MMS Email ID
Video Title: Video from My Phone
Checking one of the boxes below will append either the filename or the date to the end of your video title. This will help to make your titles unique.
☑ Filename
☐ Date
Description: video uploaded from my mobile phone
Privacy: ⦿ Public
○ Private
Tags: mobile video cellphone
Please enter tags separated by spaces.
Example: surfing beach waves
Category: News & Politics
Share:
Enter email addresses, separated by commas. Maximum 200 characters.
Insert from Address Book
Notification: ☑ Email me when video upload is complete
☑ Reply via text message when the upload is complete

? Did You Know?
You can title your video using the subject line of your MMS message.

Do not upload copyrighted, obscene or any other material which violates YouTube's Terms of Use. By creating a mobile profile, you are representing that the videos uploaded from your mobile device do not violate YouTube's Terms of Use and that you own all copyrights in the videos or have express permission from the copyright owner(s) to upload them.

Read Copyright Tips for more information about copyright and YouTube's policy.

FIGURE 4-18   When you create a new mobile profile, you are asked for information about your mobile phone and mobile provider, as well as any associated details.

14.   After your profile is set up, you can record a video with your mobile phone (or other mobile device) and then e-mail it to the address that was assigned to you in the mobile profile you created, which looks something like "xxxxx@mms.youtube.com."

NOTE   *Once your video is uploaded to YouTube, you can go to your account page and edit the information for this video.*

Chapter 5

Joining the YouTube Community

How to...

- Use playlists to save collections of favorite videos
- Keep in touch with your contacts
- Subscribe to another user's channel
- Participate in groups
- Engage in community activities, like Active Sharing, streams, and contests

Now that you've uploaded your videos and are relatively satisfied with their image quality, let's take a look at some other ways that you can interact with videos already on YouTube and how you can better share your videos with the rest of the world. To begin, we'll look at ways that you can save and organize your favorite videos on YouTube, and then you'll learn about ways that you can interact with videos uploaded by other contributors to the site. In this chapter, you'll also be spending plenty of time investigating the various community pages on the YouTube Web site, such as groups and contests, as well as special features, like streams and Active Sharing.

Working with Favorites

If you find a video on YouTube that you really like and want to make it easily (or oftenly) accessible in the future, you can simply save it as a favorite. Favorites are collections of videos that are saved to your account, unlike QuickLists, which we discussed in Chapter 4. QuickLists are temporary and only last until you quit your Web browser session or shut down your computer. Favorites, by contrast, are associated with your account, so they are accessible indefinitely or until you choose to delete them. Also, YouTube keeps track of how many times a particular video has been added as a favorite, which can increase a video's popularity and, therefore, help other people to find it easily when browsing the site (displayed underneath the video as "Favorited: 100 times," for example). By making a video your favorite, you are also helping out the member who submitted the video!

Saving a Video as a Favorite

The process of saving a video as a favorite is rather straightforward, and requires only a couple of clicks (assuming that you are already logged on to your account). Once the video is saved, you can view it at any time, remove the video from your favorites, or even copy the video to a playlist. (Playlists are discussed in "Working with Playlists" later in this chapter).

Follow these steps to save a video as a favorite:

1. Make certain that you are logged on to your account, and then locate a video that you like by searching the YouTube Web site, either using the Search box at the top of any page or browsing through lists of videos using specific criteria on the Videos or Categories page.

| **FIGURE 5-1** | The Save To Favorites link provides a fast way to keep track of videos that you like. |

2. Once you've located a video that you want to save as a favorite, click the Save To Favorites link under the video (see Figure 5-1).

3. In the Add Video To Your Favorites menu that appears underneath the video, make sure that the Favorites check box is selected, and click the OK button. At this point, do *not* use the Select A Playlist drop-down menu, which is discussed in a later section, "Working with Playlists."

Watching Favorites

Once you've saved a video as a favorite, you can go to the My Favorites area of your account and watch the video at any time.

The following steps demonstrate how to watch a video that you've saved as a favorite:

1. Click the My Account link at the top of any YouTube page.

2. Under the Video section on the My Account page, click the Favorite Videos link.

3. When you arrive at the My Favorites area of your account, you should see the list of videos that you saved as favorites. Simply click the link for the video that you want to watch.

NOTE   *As an alternate shortcut to watching videos that you've saved as a favorite, you can click the Favorites link at the bottom of most YouTube Web pages (located under the Your Account section).*

Removing Favorites

If, at any time, you would like to delete a video that you have saved as a favorite (perhaps your tastes have changed or the amount of videos in your Favorites list is getting out of control), you can access the My Favorites area of your account and remove the video (see Figure 5-2).

The following steps demonstrate how to remove a video that you've saved as a favorite:

1. Click the My Account link at the top of any YouTube page.

2. Under the Video section on the My Account page, click the Favorite Videos link.

3. When you arrive at the My Favorites area of your account, click the Remove Video button under the thumbnail for the video that you want to delete from your Favorites list. Alternately, you can select the check box to the left of each video that you want to delete, and then click the Remove Videos button at the top of the page to delete all of the selected videos at once.

FIGURE 5-2   The My Favorites area of your account provides a place to play or remove videos that you previously saved as favorites.

NOTE   *As an alternate shortcut to remove videos that you've saved as a favorite, you can simply click the Favorites link at the bottom of most YouTube Web pages (located under the Your Account section), locate the video that you want to remove from the list that appears, and click the Remove Video button as outlined in the procedure.*

Working with Playlists

Playlists are collections of your favorite videos, arranged in a queue, which you can assemble and share with others. If you are familiar with applications like Apple's iTunes, then you will recognize the concept of playlists.

Playlists can be utilized in a number of ways. For example, as you locate videos on YouTube (or as you save them as favorites), you can decide to watch these videos at a later time or all at once as a complete list—like programming an evening of TV viewing (see Figure 5-3). If you're interested in videos about cats, for example, you might track down a wide selection of videos using YouTube's Search feature, add them to a playlist you've set up, and then sit back and watch the entire show unfold. In addition, if you have a large number of videos on your own YouTube channel, you can use playlists to organize these videos according to any criteria that you want. For example, you might create a playlist called Music Videos and another called Interviews to hold the corresponding types of videos that you've uploaded. If you have a lot of videos, this can

My Account / Playlists

My Videos - Favorites - Playlists - Inbox - more ▼

My Videos
My Remixed Videos
My Favorites
My Top Videos - 2

Create Playlist
Upload a Video

▶ **My Top Videos**
Description:

Edit   Delete Playlist   Set as Video Log

URL: http://www.youtube.com/view_play_list?p=5E6E5
Embed: <object width="530" height="370"> <param nam

▶ Play All Videos   ✉ Share This Playlist

Remove Videos | Copy Videos To: ----------- ▼   Rearrange

AMERICA   1
03:09
A Brief History of Television, Religion, Sports, Politics, War, Censorship, and Other Favorite
American Pastimes

Public Domain (more)
        Edit Description   Make Playlist Icon
Remove Video
        Added: November 18, 2006, 10:05 PM
        From: chadfahs
        Views: 397
        Rating: ★★★★☆
            2 ratings

funny cats   2
01:38
funny cats
        Edit Description   Make Playlist Icon
Remove Video
        Added: December 20, 2005, 05:19 AM
        From: neverende
        Views: 12,970,710
        Rating: ★★★★☆
            22933 ratings

Remove Videos | Copy Videos To: ----------- ▼   Rearrange

FIGURE 5-3 Playlists are a great way to organize your favorite videos for later playback or
sharing with friends.

make it easier for viewers of your channel to locate the videos that they want to watch. You can
create as many playlists as you need, and can edit or delete them at any time. In addition, you can
add your playlists to other Web sites and share them with friends.

Creating a Playlist

Creating a playlist is similar to saving a favorite. In fact, playlists are really just organized lists of
your favorite videos.

The following steps demonstrate how to create a playlist using the most direct method:

1. Locate a video that you like by searching the YouTube Web site, either using the Search
   box at the top of any page or browsing through lists of videos using specific criteria on
   the Videos or Categories page.

2. Once you've located a video that you want to add to a playlist, click the Save To
   Favorites link under the video.

3. Choose New Playlist from the Add Video To A Playlist drop-down menu that appears under the video.

4. Click the OK button. The video is now added to a new playlist, and the Create/Edit Playlist page appears.

5. Enter a name for the playlist in the Playlist Name text box, fill in the Description field, add any tags that you might want to help users find your playlist better when conducting searches, and then select whether you want the playlist to be public or private by selecting the relevant check box.

6. When you are done entering information, click the Save Playlist Info button. You will return to the original page with the video that you just saved to your playlist.

Alternately, you might choose to create a new playlist from the My Account area of your YouTube account first before using the Save To Favorites button on a particular video. In this way, you can set up and create a playlist as an empty container prior to adding your favorite videos. When you are ready to save a video as a favorite, the playlist you set up in advance will be available through the Add Video To A Playlist drop-down menu you encountered in the last procedure.

The following steps demonstrate how to add a video to a playlist that is created in advance, which is similar to what you did in the previous procedure, except in reverse order (you are setting up the playlist first before searching and locating a video to add):

1. Click the My Account link at the top of any YouTube page.

2. Under the Video section on the My Account page, click the Playlists link.

3. Click the Create Playlist button on the left side of the page, or click the Create Playlist button in the middle of the page, which appears if you haven't already created a playlist.

4. Enter a name for the playlist in the Playlist Name text box, fill in the Description field, add any tags you might want, and then select whether you want the playlist to be public or private by selecting the relevant check box.

NOTE   *The Use This Playlist As My Video Log In My Channel option simply means that you'd like to add this playlist to your vlog (video Web log) or channel. Any playlists that you select this option for will appear on your channel page. If you decide that you want to use this option later on, you can activate it from the main playlist page by clicking the Set As Video Log button for the corresponding playlist.*

5. When you are done entering information, click the Save Playlist Info button. You will return to the Playlists page of your account.

6. Locate a video that you like by searching the YouTube Web site either using the Search box at the top of any page or browsing through lists of videos using specific criteria on the Videos or Categories page.

7. Once you've located a video that you want to add to a playlist, click the Save To Favorites link under the video.

8. Choose the name of the playlist you created from the Add Video To A Playlist drop-down menu that appears under the video.

9. Click the OK button. The video is now added to the new playlist.

Watching a Playlist

After you have created a playlist, particularly if that playlist has several videos in it, you may choose to watch it in its entirety. Of course, you can choose to watch individual videos in your playlist as well, just as you did for favorites.

Watching a playlist is simple and can be achieved by performing the following steps:

1. Click the My Account link at the top of any YouTube page.

2. Under the Video section on the My Account page, click the Playlists link.

3. On the left side of the Playlist's page, click the link for the playlist you want to view.

4. In the blue bar at the top of your selected playlist, click the Play button next to the name of the playlist, or click the Play All Videos button. You will automatically be taken to the page for the first video in the playlist. Once that video has finished playing, the next video in the playlist will automatically play, and so on, until each of the videos in your playlist has been viewed.

NOTE
As an alternate shortcut to watching a playlist you've created, you can click the Playlists link at the bottom of most YouTube Web pages (located under the Your Account section).

Editing, Rearranging, and Deleting Items from a Playlist

Once you've created one or more playlists, you might decide to delete items from one of the playlists, rearrange items in the playlist, or simply remove an entire playlist altogether. The following steps demonstrate how to edit a playlist and perform these simple functions:

1. Click the My Account link at the top of any YouTube page.

2. Under the Video section on the My Account page, click the Playlists link.

3. On the left side of the Playlist's page, click the link for the playlist you want to view. If you have more than one playlist, you should notice separate links for each of them.

4. If you want to change any information for your playlist, click the Edit button in the blue bar at the top of your selected playlist.

5. On the Create/Edit Playlist page that appears, you can modify any information that you want (such as playlist name, description, tags, and privacy settings), and then click Save Playlist Info to apply the changes. After clicking Save Playlist Info, you are automatically returned to the main Playlists page.

6. On the main Playlists page, you can rearrange items in the playlist by entering a different number in the box on the right side of each video item and then clicking the Rearrange button at the top or bottom of the playlist. The number that is added to each item determines the order in which the videos play back when viewing the entire playlist (all videos are sorted into their new numerical order until you choose to rearrange them again).

7. If you decide that you would rather remove certain videos from the playlist, you can click the Remove Video button under that particular video's thumbnail in the playlist, or you can select the check box located to the left of the video's thumbnail and then click the Remove Videos button at the top or bottom of the playlist. In this way, you can remove multiple videos at once by selecting several check boxes for different videos in the playlist.

8. If you decide to delete the entire playlist, you can click the Delete Playlist button, and when the confirmation dialog box appears, simply click OK.

NOTE   *As mentioned previously, you can use an alternate shortcut to accessing a playlist you've created by clicking the Playlists link at the bottom of most YouTube Web pages (located under the Your Account section).*

Copying Videos to a Playlist

If you have several videos saved as favorites and would like to add them to a playlist, or if you have videos in one playlist that you'd like to move to another playlist, you can use the Copy Videos To command in either your My Favorites or My Playlists page (see Figure 5-4).

The following steps demonstrate how to copy videos from your Favorites list to a playlist or from one playlist to another playlist:

1. Click the My Account link at the top of any YouTube page.

2. Under the Video section on the My Account page, click the Favorite Videos link or the Playlists link.

3. Select the check box to the left of any video item (or multiple video items) in your Favorites list or selected playlist.

FIGURE 5-4   The Copy Videos To command allows you to move videos from one playlist to another.

4. In the Copy Videos To drop-down menu, select the name of the playlist you would like to copy the videos to, or choose New Playlist to add them to a new playlist that you create (as outlined in the earlier section "Creating a Playlist").

NOTE   *As mentioned previously, you can use an alternate shortcut to accessing a playlist you've created by clicking the Playlists link at the bottom of most YouTube Web pages (located under the Your Account section).*

Searching for Playlists

If you're interested in a particular subject or theme, rather than searching for random videos scattered across YouTube (which may or may not be relevant to your interests), why not search for a playlist that's already been assembled with handpicked videos (see Figure 5-5)?

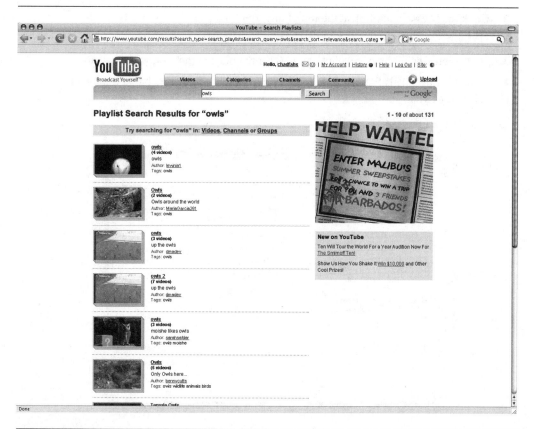

FIGURE 5-5   Playlists also appear as criteria in search results.

Follow these steps to locate a playlist you want to watch:

1. Use the Search box, located at the top of each YouTube page, to search for a specific keyword in the playlist that you want to find.

2. When the search results are returned, click the Playlists link on the left side of the page. All of the playlists that have those terms will appear, and may be sorted further using the Sort By criteria on the left side of the page, such as by date added, view count, or rating.

Sharing Playlists

If you have created a playlist that you'd like to share with friends or family, you can use the Share This Playlist option, which allows you to send a simple message to e-mail addresses that you specify, including a link to the playlist that you want to share (see Figure 5-6).

The following steps demonstrate how to share a playlist that you have created:

1. Click the My Account link at the top of any YouTube page.

2. Under the Video section on the My Account page, click the Playlists link.

3. On the left side of the page, click the link for the playlist that you want to share.

4. Click the Share This Playlist link, located on the right of the blue bar at the top of the selected playlist.

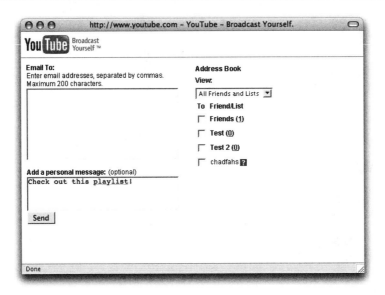

FIGURE 5-6   You can share playlists with friends and family by providing some basic information.

5. In the pop-up window that opens, enter the e-mail addresses of the people you want to send this message to with a link to the playlist. A comma should separate all e-mail addresses, and you may include a maximum of 200 characters in the E-mail To text box (which limits the number of people you can send to at one time, helping to avoid spam).

6. Type a message about the playlist you are sending in the Add A Personal Message (optional) text box.

7. When you are done filling in information for your message, click the Send button. The window will display a thumbnail for your playlist, with a message that states, "The playlist has been sent successfully." You may close this window. At this point, an e-mail is sent to the addresses you specified, with a link to your playlist. The e-mail is sent from service@youtube.com, which is how it will appear in your recipients' e-mail inboxes.

Managing Your Friends and Contacts

On YouTube, "friends" are the people with whom you share your videos and messages (see Figure 5-7). For example, when you find a video that you like, you can easily share it with a large group of people that you've added as your friends. Also, whenever you share a video or playlist with someone, their e-mail address is automatically added to your list of contacts. Of course, you can also set up your contact list ahead of time—that way, you can send messages without taking the time to type addresses. If your friend has a channel on YouTube, you can add them as a friend through their profile page (which is similar to MySpace). You may also search for people to add as a friend by using the See If Your Friends Are Already On YouTube Search box on the Friends & Contacts page of your account.

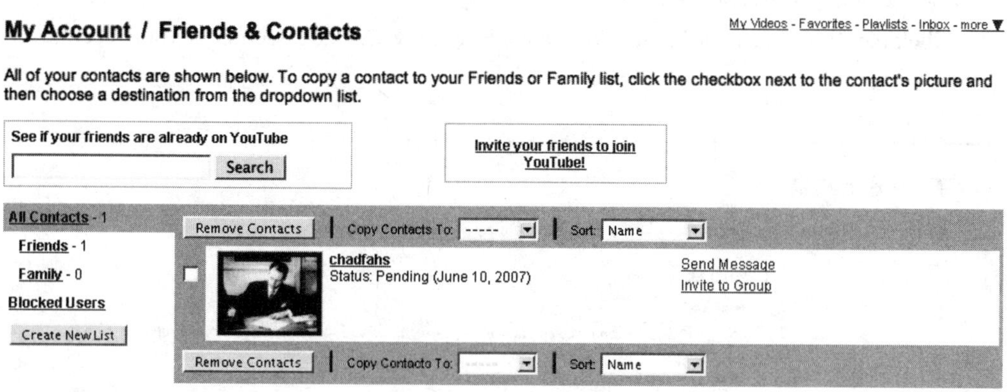

My Account / Friends & Contacts

My Videos - Favorites - Playlists - Inbox - more ▼

All of your contacts are shown below. To copy a contact to your Friends or Family list, click the checkbox next to the contact's picture and then choose a destination from the dropdown list.

See if your friends are already on YouTube [   ] Search

Invite your friends to join YouTube!

All Contacts - 1
Friends - 1
Family - 0
Blocked Users
Create New List

Remove Contacts | Copy Contacts To: ----- ▼ | Sort: Name ▼

☐ **chadfahs**
Status: Pending (June 10, 2007)

Send Message
Invite to Group

Remove Contacts | Copy Contacts To: ----- ▼ | Sort: Name ▼

FIGURE 5-7   YouTube provides different ways to manage contacts for your account.

Adding a Friend

Adding someone you know on YouTube as a friend is easy to do. Just make sure that the person is someone you want to include on all of your posts. Otherwise, you may want to restrict what you send to them if it's too personal. Once again, if you are familiar with sites like MySpace or Facebook, then you are probably aware of the protocol regarding "friends."

Follow these steps to add a friend to your contact list:

1. Make certain that you are logged on to your account.
2. Navigate the channel of a user that you want to add as a friend, such as www.youtube .com/chadfahs.
3. In the Connect With section of this person's channel, click the Add As Friend link.
4. On the Friend Invitation page that appears, choose Friend or Family from the Add As drop-down menu (see Figure 5-8).
5. Click the Send Invite button to complete the process. After clicking this button, you are returned to the Friends & Contacts page of your account. A "friend" has to accept your invitation in order to appear as a valid contact and for you to interact with them further.

Removing a Friend

Maybe it's inevitable, but at some point, you might need to remove someone from your contacts. Perhaps they have stopped using their account, changed to a new account, or you simply do not want to include them in your private posts anymore. Whatever the reason, removing a friend is simple.

1. Make certain that you are logged on to your account, and click the My Account button at the top of any YouTube page.
2. Click the All Contacts or Friends link in the Friends & Contacts section of your account.

Friend Invitation

Send an invitation if you know this user and wish to share private videos with each other.

Username: chadfahs
Add As: [--- ▼]
This person will be able to see the private videos you share with these groups in addition to your public videos.

[Send Invite]

FIGURE 5-8   It's easy to add a friend using the Add As Friend button on a user's channel.

3. In the contacts list that appears, select the check box next to the contact that you want to remove.

4. Click the Remove Contacts button, and then click OK to complete the process. A dialog box will appear, confirming that you want to perform this action.

Creating a New Contacts List

In addition to using the standard "Friends" and "Family" contact lists, you may also create custom lists through your My Account page to better organize friends into different groups. For example, you might create a "School" list and a "Work" list, which will make it easier when you just want to send a video or message to a select group from your entire contacts list.

Follow these steps to create a new contacts list:

1. Make certain that you are logged on to your account, and click the My Account button at the top of any YouTube page.

2. Click the All Contacts link in the Friends & Contacts section of your account.

3. On the left side of the Friends & Contacts page, at the bottom of your contacts list, click the Create New List button.

4. In the pop-up window that opens, follow the directions to enter a name for a new contact group. The name can be anything you want, such as the aforementioned "School," "Work," or something even more specific (see Figure 5-9). The choice is yours.

5. When you are done entering a name, click the OK button. You will see the new list name appear under your existing contact groups on the left side of the page.

The page at http://www.youtube.com says:

Enter a name for a new contact group.

School Contacts List

Cancel   OK

FIGURE 5-9   Creating a new list to organize your contacts helps you send videos, messages, and other YouTube communications to the right people.

Creating and Managing Subscriptions

Subscribing to a YouTube channel is a great way to keep tabs on the latest videos by your favorite YouTube members. Perhaps there is a YouTube series that a particular channel produces, or maybe it's just a lone user who has something interesting to say. Either way, by subscribing to another member's channel, you can keep informed of any videos that they upload and generally manage the videos that they have already uploaded. Whenever a new video is uploaded, you will receive an e-mail that tells you it is available for viewing. (You can turn this feature off for a particular channel by clicking Remove From E-mail Update in the My Subscriptions area of your account.) By using the Subscriptions & Subscribers area of your account, you can manage channels that you are subscribed to, as well as the users that are subscribed to you.

Subscribing to Other Users

As you watch and browse videos on YouTube, you may notice that a particular YouTube member has a lot of interesting videos that appeal to you. In this case, you might decide to subscribe to their channel so that you are automatically notified when they upload new videos.

The following steps demonstrate how to subscribe to another user's channel:

1. Locate the video or the channel of a user that you want to subscribe to.

2. Click the orange Subscribe button in the information area for the video or its channel (see Figure 5-10). The channel is automatically added to your subscriptions, and you are taken to the My Subscriptions area of your account. You will be notified whenever new content is posted to this user's channel.

TIP *You may also subscribe to videos based on a particular set of tags that are associated with them. For example, you can subscribe to all of the channels that have the words "3D," "Animation," and "Art" added to them. Simply enter the tags you desire into the Subscribe To Tags text box at the top of your My Subscriptions page for your account, and click the Subscribe button.*

FIGURE 5-10   You can subscribe to another user's channel by simply clicking the Subscribe button.

FIGURE 5-11   Unsubscribing is as easy as subscribing.

Unsubscribing from a Channel

If you are no longer interested in a particular channel, you can easily remove it from your subscriptions. Of course, as a content creator on YouTube, you want other users to subscribe to your channel, not unsubscribe. In order to keep your subscribers happy, be sure to upload some cool content every now and then!

Follow these steps to unsubscribe from a channel:

1. Click the My Account link at the top of any YouTube page.

2. Under the Subscriptions & Subscribers section on the My Account page, click the My Subscriptions link.

3. On the My Subscriptions page, click the link for the channel that you want to remove.

4. At the top of the channel's listing, click the Unsubscribe button to remove it from your subscriptions (see Figure 5-11).

> **NOTE**   *You can also unsubscribe from a channel by visiting its page and clicking the gray Unsubscribe button, exactly where you had previously found the orange Subscribe button. Also, even though you may have already subscribed to a user's channel, you may still see a Subscribe button when watching their individual videos.*

Viewing Subscriptions

Now that you have subscribed to a few channels, you can quickly sort through and view the videos as they are uploaded using the My Subscriptions area of your account (see Figure 5-12). In particular, the most useful feature is probably New Videos, which allows you to look at only the latest videos that have been added, rather than having to sift through all of the older videos for a channel, or through multiple channels, to find them.

The following steps describe the basic ways to view videos for channels that you are subscribed to:

1. Click the My Account link at the top of any YouTube page.

2. Under the Subscriptions & Subscribers section on the My Account page, click the My Subscriptions link.

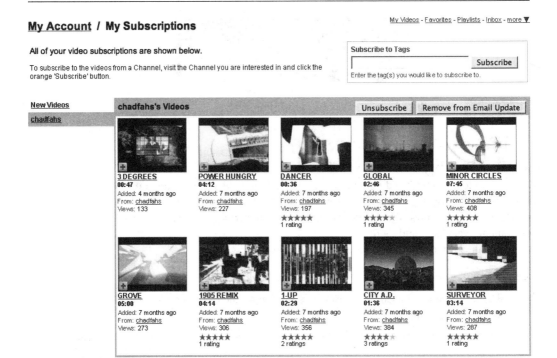

My Videos - Favorites - Playlists - Inbox - more ▼

My Account / My Subscriptions

All of your video subscriptions are shown below.

To subscribe to the videos from a Channel, visit the Channel you are interested in and click the orange 'Subscribe' button.

Subscribe to Tags

[   ] [Subscribe]

Enter the tag(s) you would like to subscribe to.

New Videos

chadfahs

chadfahs's Videos   [Unsubscribe] [Remove from Email Update]

3 DEGREES
00:47
Added: 4 months ago
From: chadfahs
Views: 133

POWER HUNGRY
04:12
Added: 7 months ago
From: chadfahs
Views: 227

DANCER
00:36
Added: 7 months ago
From: chadfahs
Views: 197
★★★★★
1 rating

GLOBAL
02:46
Added: 7 months ago
From: chadfahs
Views: 345
★★★★★
1 rating

MINOR CIRCLES
07:45
Added: 7 months ago
From: chadfahs
Views: 408
★★★★★
1 rating

GROVE
05:00
Added: 7 months ago
From: chadfahs
Views: 273
★★★★★
1 rating

1905 REMIX
04:14
Added: 7 months ago
From: chadfahs
Views: 306
★★★★★
1 rating

1-UP
02:29
Added: 7 months ago
From: chadfahs
Views: 356
★★★★★
2 ratings

CITY A.D.
01:36
Added: 7 months ago
From: chadfahs
Views: 384
★★★★★
3 ratings

SURVEYOR
03:14
Added: 7 months ago
From: chadfahs
Views: 287
★★★★★
1 rating

FIGURE 5-12   You can manage subscriptions through the My Subscriptions area of your account page, including viewing and removing subscriptions.

3. Click the New Videos button that appears at the top of your subscriptions list to see only the latest videos that have been added from all of the channels that you are subscribed to.

4. To see the contents of a particular channel, click its name to view the first several videos with their respective thumbnails.

5. Click a video thumbnail or link to play a video as you ordinarily would.

Removing Subscribers to Your Channel

On rare occasions, you may have someone subscribe to your channel who you do not want included in your e-mails regarding new uploads or want visible on your channel to others as a subscriber. Perhaps he or she is someone who has been verbally abusive in comments left for your videos or in forums. Whatever the reason, it is quite simple to remove a subscriber to your channel.

The following steps describe how to remove a subscriber to your channel:

1. Click the My Account link at the top of any YouTube page.

2. Under the Subscriptions & Subscribers section on the My Account page, click the My Subscribers link. A list of all the users who are subscribed to your channel will appear.

3. Click the Unsubscribe button that appears underneath the name of the subscribers you want to remove.

Using Comments

Whenever you have something to say about a video that you watch on YouTube, whether it's a comment about how much you like it or a criticism of its content, you can post a comment. Anyone who visits the video's page on YouTube may view and (in turn) respond with their own comment as well. Comments have become commonplace on blogs and networking sites like MySpace or Facebook. As mentioned, they can be used to start a conversation about the merits of particular videos or to correct some misunderstanding about the video's content. Unfortunately, comments sometimes turn into forums for childish name-calling or (worse still) another avenue for spammers to exploit. In this case, it is also useful to be able to remove comments from your videos if you need to.

Posting and Replying to Text Comments on a Video

It's easy to post a text comment to a video, or even to a user's channel (see Figure 5-13). Of course, before posting your comment, make sure that it doesn't violate any of the decency standards of the site and that it doesn't reflect poorly on you or your identity on YouTube (especially if you use your real name, like I do). With some common sense, comments (whether on YouTube or a blog) can be a useful way for people to interact and exchange ideas online.

The following steps demonstrate how to post text comments to a video that you've found on YouTube:

1. Locate a video that you want to add a text comment to, provided you have something insightful to say!

2. Click the Post A Text Comment link beneath the video, or simply scroll down until you see the Comment On This Video text box at the bottom of the page.

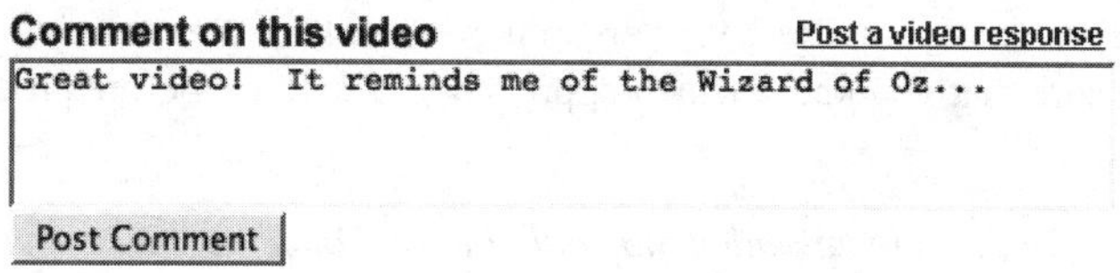

Comment on this video   <u>Post a video response</u>

Great video!   It reminds me of the Wizard of Oz...

Post Comment

FIGURE 5-13   Post a comment when you have something you'd like to say about a video.

3. In the Text Comments field that appears (or in the Comment On This Video text box), type your comment.

4. When you are done typing, click the Post Comment button to apply your comment to the video.

5. To reorder the comments as you see them, click Most Recent or Oldest to determine the order in which they appear (top to bottom or bottom to top). By default (at least when you add a new video to your channel), the newest comments appear underneath.

6. When someone leaves a comment on one of your videos and you want to respond, simply click Reply below the comment, fill in the text box that appears, and click Post Comment when you are ready to post it (or click Discard if you change your mind).

Adding Comments to a Channel

Adding comments to a user's channel is essentially the same as posting them to a video you find on YouTube. The main difference is that comments added to a channel are usually targeted at the creator, not a specific video. They are also placed on the main channel page, and the form that you fill out to place them is slightly different.

If you want to add a comment to a user's channel, follow these steps:

1. Locate a channel that you want to add a text comment to.

2. Click the Add Comment link in the Connect With box, or click on the Comments box on the page.

3. In the Post A New Comment box that appears, type your comment. At this point, you may also choose to attach a video, which is discussed in the next section, "Posting a Video Response."

4. When you are done typing, click the Submit Comment button to apply your comment to the channel.

Posting a Video Response

In addition to text comments, video responses may be added to a video or a channel. Essentially, a video response is what it sounds like—a comment in the form of a video that is attached to another video. The video response may be a video you have already uploaded, a video that you are about to upload, or you can choose to create a video on the spot using Quick Capture. A video response may also be used to direct viewers to the "sequel" of another video or to videos in a series. Just make sure that you know which approach you will use before proceeding with the post.

NOTE *A video you have already uploaded may only be used once as a video response on YouTube.*

Post a Video Response

Responding to: 1905 REMIX

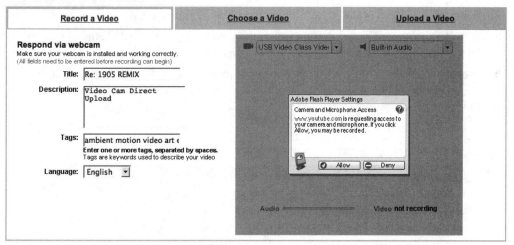

Ever wanted to talk back to a video? Now's your chance—you can upload a response to this video and we will link them together. You can record a new video, choose from the videos you already have, or create and upload a new video.

Record a Video	Choose a Video	Upload a Video

Respond via webcam
Make sure your webcam is installed and working correctly.
(All fields need to be entered before recording can begin)

Title: Re: 1905 REMIX

Description: Video Cam Direct Upload

Tags: ambient motion video art e
Enter one or more tags, separated by spaces.
Tags are keywords used to describe your video

Language: English

USB Video Class Vide   Built-in Audio

Adobe Flash Player Settings
Camera and Microphone Access
www.youtube.com is requesting access to your camera and microphone. If you click Allow, you may be recorded.

Allow   Deny

Audio   Video **not recording**

FIGURE 5-14   You can post a video response in three different ways.

The following steps demonstrate how to post a video response to a video on YouTube:

1. Locate a video on YouTube that you want to post a video response to.

2. Click the Post A Video Response link beneath the video. The Video Response page appears.

3. On the Video Response page, you may choose to record a video using a webcam and the Quick Capture feature, choose a video that you have already uploaded, or upload a new video (see Figure 5-14). Follow the steps for the option you have chosen to complete the video response. If you decide to record a video, make certain that you follow the steps for Quick Capture, which are outlined in Chapter 4. You will first need to click the Allow button if you want to give YouTube access to the webcam that is attached to your computer.

Posting a Bulletin

Every now and then, you might want to communicate with the people who visit your channel. For example, you might want to let them know that you have a new Web series in the works or that you will be adding more videos soon. You can do this easily by posting a bulletin to your profile.

When someone visits your channel, they will see a link to the message that you created in the Bulletins area of the page (see Figure 5-15).

Follow these steps to post a bulletin to your channel:

1. Make certain that you are logged on to your account, and then navigate to your channel (profile) page.

2. In the Bulletins area of the page, click the Broadcast A Message link.

3. A Bulletin Post page appears, where you can enter a subject for your bulletin, as well as attach a video and fill in the body of your message.

4. When you are done filling out the Bulletin Post page, click the Post Bulletin button. If you return to your channel page, you will now see a new bulletin (date and title, with link) in the Bulletins area.

FIGURE 5-15   Bulletins let everyone know the latest news about your channel.

Sending Messages

Once you have some contacts added to your account (as discussed earlier in this chapter), whether they belong to Friends, Family, or some other group, you can easily send them a personal message from your YouTube account (see Figure 5-16). As opposed to a comment or a bulletin, messages are only visible to the contacts you've sent it to (they are notified by e-mail that a message is waiting for them in their account).

Follow these steps to send a message to a contact:

1. Make certain that you are logged on to your account, and click the My Account button at the top of any YouTube page.

2. Click the All Contacts or Friends link in the Friends & Contacts section of your My Account page.

3. Locate the contact that you want to send a message to, and then click the Send Message button to the right of the person's name.

4. In the Compose Message page that appears, enter a subject line for your message, choose whether you want to attach a video, and type your message in the Message area.

5. When you are finished composing your message, click Send Message.

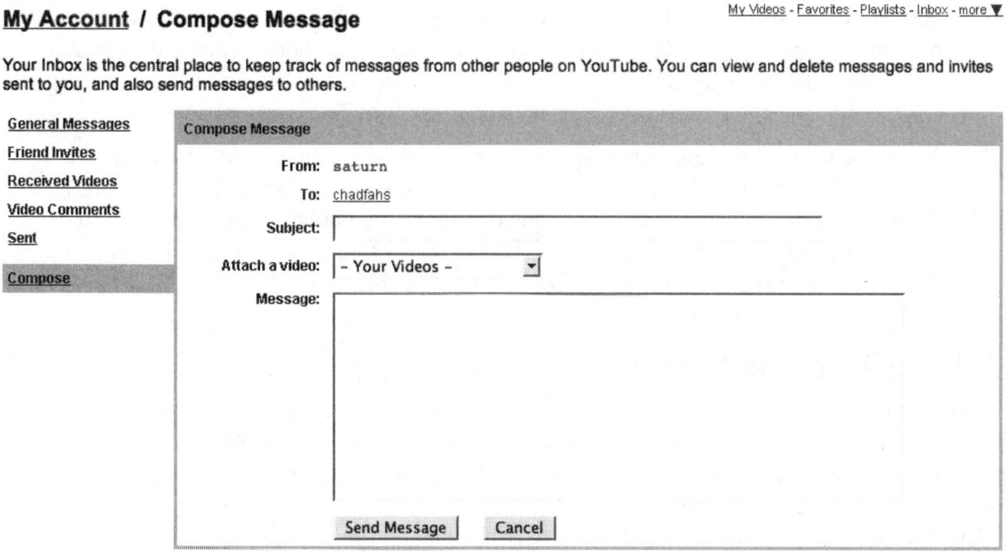

My Account / Compose Message   My Videos - Favorites - Playlists - Inbox - more ▼

Your Inbox is the central place to keep track of messages from other people on YouTube. You can view and delete messages and invites sent to you, and also send messages to others.

General Messages	**Compose Message**
Friend Invites	
Received Videos	From: saturn
Video Comments	To: chadfahs
Sent	Subject: [ ]
Compose	Attach a video: [– Your Videos – ▼]
	Message: [ ]
	[Send Message] [Cancel]

FIGURE 5-16   Compose messages when you want to send a personal note to someone, as with an e-mail.

Working with YouTube Groups

A great way to interact with other users and generate discussion on YouTube is to create a group. YouTube groups are special places where members can discuss topics, make comments, and post videos that are relevant to the group. In addition, groups are often used for contests by various companies and commercial entities. Groups can be large or small, and you can join one that is already in operation or start your own. If your interest is photography, for example, you can find several groups that match those criteria, or you can create one. Providing a forum to exchange videos and ideas related to a specific set of interests (and a system that is opted into by individual members) helps you to get your videos seen, meet people with similar interests, or find other videos that match your personal preferences.

Browsing for Groups

The first step to learning about groups is to take a look at a few. The easiest way to browse the groups that are available is to go directly to the Groups area of YouTube. You can find groups within the Community portion of the site (see Figure 5-17).

Follow these steps to browse through groups on YouTube:

1. Click the Community tab, located at the top of most YouTube pages.

2. Click the Groups link, located on the left side of the Community page.

3. On the left side of the page, notice the variety of browsing and category criteria, and then click one of the links to sort the search results for groups. For example, you might choose to search for groups with the most members. You might also choose to view different groups according to categories (as you might with videos), such as Entertainment, Film & Animation, or Travel & Places, to name just a few.

4. When you've located a group that appeals to you, click its thumbnail or link to view more details about the group. Notice that at the top of the group's page, the number of videos, members, and discussions associated with this particular group are listed. All of the details regarding those categories, as well as access to the videos (including recent videos as featured) and discussions, may be found on this page.

Joining a YouTube Group

In order to learn more about groups and what they really have to offer, you should start by joining at least one. Joining a group allows you to do things like upload videos to the group and participate in discussions. After you've got your feet wet participating in an existing group, you may decide to start one of your own.

The following steps demonstrate how to subscribe to a YouTube group:

1. Search for a group that you'd like to join by entering keywords into the Search box at the top or bottom of any YouTube page, and then filter the results by clicking Groups in the column on the left of the page. You may also browse for groups using the method described in the previous section, "Browsing for Groups."

FIGURE 5-17   Groups are found in the Community section of YouTube.

2. Click the thumbnail or link for a particular group to access the details about it.

3. Click the Join This Group link in the upper-right corner of the page to join. If at any time you want to leave the group, simply click the Leave This Group link, which appears in the same area of the page after you join.

Creating a YouTube Group

After you've had a chance to explore various groups on YouTube, you might decide to create one for a topic that interests you. The following steps demonstrate how to create a new YouTube group:

1. Click the Community tab, located at the top of most YouTube pages.

2. Click the Groups link, located on the left side of the Community page.

3. On the Groups page, click the Create A Group button, located on the left side of the page, under the list of categories.

4. On the Create A Group page that appears, fill in the name you want for your group in the Group Name text box (see Figure 5-18).

5. Continue to fill out the Create A Group page by adding a list of tags and a description.

6. Enter a custom Uniform Resource Locator (URL) for your group in the Choose A Unique Group Name URL field. As noted on the page, you can enter 3 to 18 characters with no spaces. The text you enter will become part of your group's Web address. The group name URL that you pick is permanent and can't be changed.

7. Under Group Category, select the one option that most closely matches the subject matter of your group, such as Film & Animation or Pets & Animals.

8. Decide what privacy setting you want to apply to this group. Your choices are Public, Anyone Can Join; Protected, Requires Founder Approval To Join; or Private, By Founder Invite Only, Only Members Can View Group Details.

9. Under the Video Uploads section, choose Post Videos Immediately, Founder Approval Required Before Video Is Available; or Only Founder Can Add New Videos. These options are particularly important if you want to control the type of content that is uploaded, especially if you wish to censor any videos.

10. Finish filling out the form by choosing options in the Forum Postings area (the options are the same as in the Video Uploads section), and in the Group Icon area, which is the picture that is displayed as your group's thumbnail (your choices are Automatically Set Group Icon To Last Uploaded Video or Let Owner Pick The Video As Group Icon).

11. When you are done with this form, click Create Group. Your new group page appears and is completely empty at this point. It's up to you to begin adding some content, including adding a video or new topic (type some thoughts about the group's subject matter, and then click the Add Topic button to get the discussion going).

Once you've created a group, you can further manage it by clicking the Groups link at the top of your channel (profile) page (or by accessing the My Groups area through your account page), selecting a group from the list you've created, and then choosing Edit Group Details, Manage Videos, Add Videos, Invite Members, or Disable Notifications.

TIP *You can transfer the ownership of a group you create to another user, who will take over your duties as the owner or moderator of the group. Once you've accessed a group through your profile page, click the Edit Group Details link, and then scroll to the bottom of the page to find the Click Here To Transfer Ownership Of This Group To Another User option under the Update Group button.*

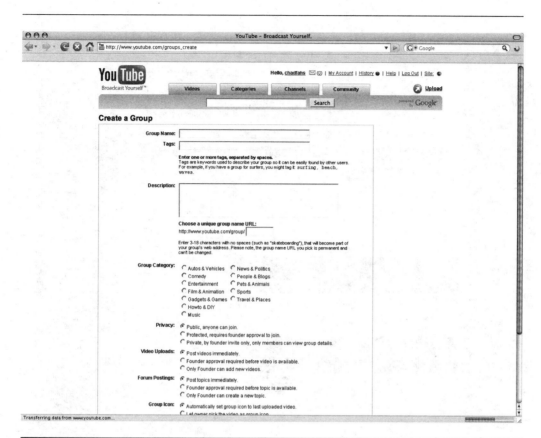

The Create A Group page is where you can set up and customize the parameters for your own group.

Joining Your College

Similar to joining a general group, you can join a special group for your college. If your alma mater is on YouTube, you'll find it by going to the Community tab and clicking either Groups or Colleges under the Browse section. You can then select your college from the list that appears and click Join Now (see Figure 5-19). In order to sign up, however, you need to have an e-mail address from your college (many colleges offer e-mail addresses to alumni as well).

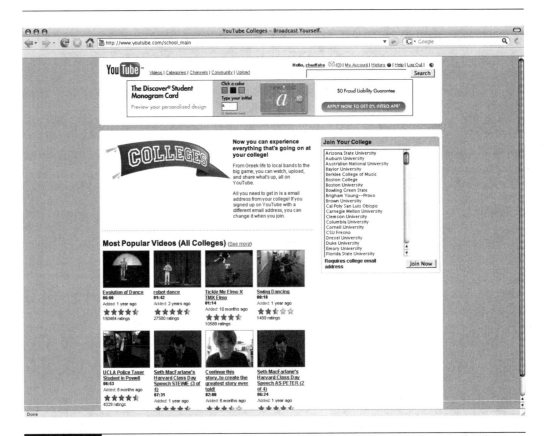

FIGURE 5-19   Joining a college group is a great way to see what other students or faculty are up to on YouTube.

Participating in Contests

There are several other ways to participate in the YouTube community apart from groups. One of the ways you can get involved is by engaging in one of the contests that YouTube frequently lists on the site. Open contests are listed on the Community portion of YouTube (see Figure 5-20). Simply click the Community tab, located at the top of most pages, and select Contests from the list on the left side of the page (contests are sometimes also listed within the Groups portion of the site). View the details for available contests and then submit videos that match that contest's requirements. Contests are often sponsored by large corporations, such as Samsung.

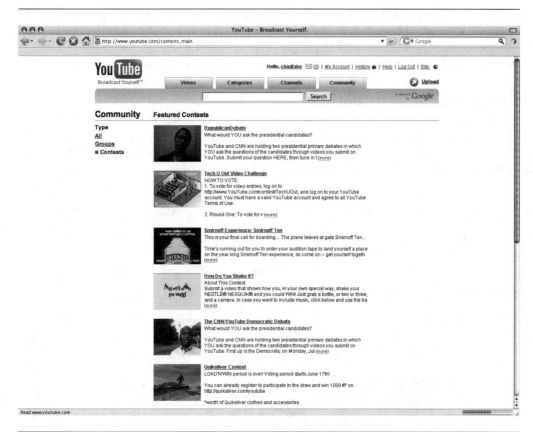

Contests are a unique way to get noticed (and maybe even earn some money) on YouTube.

Participating in a Stream

Streams are another innovative community feature of the YouTube Web site and are still (at the time of this writing) part of the TestTube functionality of the site (functions and layout are subject to change), as shown in Figure 5-21. Basically, *streams* are rooms where videos are

Streams
Join Streams to chat with others who are watching the same video you are.
Try it out | Feedback?

Streams are one of the newer features of the YouTube Web site and are currently accessed through the TestTube link.

played live while people chat and discuss the videos with other users. Participants in a stream can also add their own video selections for others to see, such as videos from their Favorites list, QuickLinks, or pasted links. It's like participating in a public screening or film club, where participants can discuss the videos as they are playing, and each has their turn to play VJ.

Joining and Viewing a Stream

You can join a stream by invitation (where someone sends you an invitation to join by clicking the Invite button) or by browsing available streams at www.youtube.com/streams_main and choosing one from the list (see Figure 5-22). Once you click the stream you want to participate in, you will be presented with the Streams window.

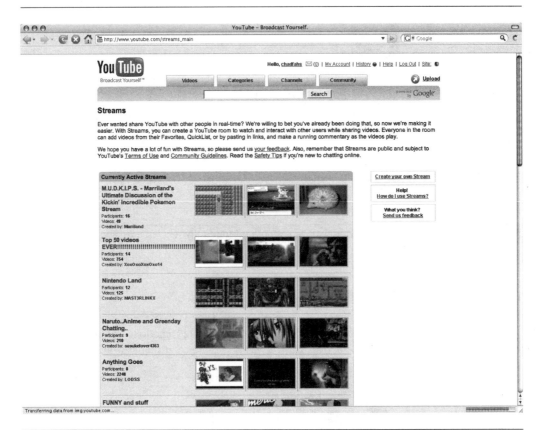

FIGURE 5-22   Streams are a lively way to watch and comment on videos with other users in real time.

Streams are broken into two areas: video and chat. The videos that play in a stream are shown on the left side of the page, and the chat that ensues is shown on the right. In the Stream Library portion of the page, you will see video thumbnails and links for each of the videos that are a part of that particular stream. Clicking one of these videos loads it into the player. You can add to the available videos by using the Add To Stream area of the page, which you can expand, and then locate videos in a variety of ways (options include Search, My Videos, My Favorites, or URL).

Every user who is currently participating in the stream is listed on the right, along with their chat and comments as they are posted (like group instant-messaging). If you want to add to the conversation, simply type in the text box and click Post. Your comments will appear on the page with everyone else's, along with a thumbnail of the video that you are currently watching.

> **NOTE**   *Conversations in streams occur in real time and, as a result, their messages have not been screened for appropriate content. This is particularly important when considering use of streams by underage YouTubers. Also, be careful to not reveal any personal information during a streaming session that may help another user to identify your age, location, or other details that may result in safety concerns.*

Creating a Stream

It's not difficult to create your own stream. In fact, it can be a lot of fun to start a live discussion with other users. Perhaps you will decide to create a stream that's designed for you and your friends to meet (kind of like a virtual video clubhouse), or maybe you'll leave it open to anyone who wants to participate.

> **NOTE**   *YouTube has a limit on the number of streams that can be active at any given time, so it may not be always possible to create a stream when you want it.*

The following steps discuss how to create a new stream:

1. Click the TestTube link at the bottom of any YouTube page, and then click the Streams button.

2. On the Streams page that appears, click the Create Your Own Streams link on the right side of the page.

3. On the Create/Edit Stream page that appears, customize the preferences for your new stream, including adding a background image (to make the stream more inviting based on your theme), a welcome message, and parameters for the maximum number of users (300 is the limit), the number of flags to remove a video (for videos that are flagged as inappropriate by viewers), and who can add videos to this stream (see Figure 5-23).

4. When you are done filling out the form on the Create/Edit Stream page, click Save Stream Info. You are now ready to begin using the stream.

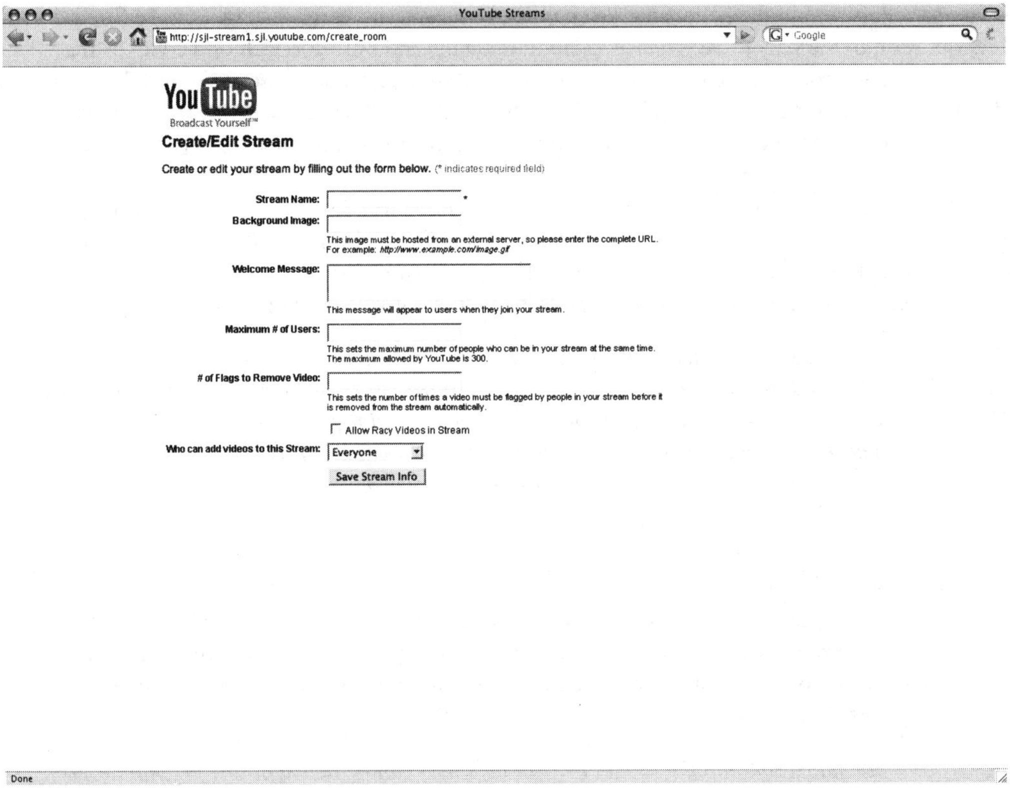

FIGURE 5-23 The Create/Edit Stream page is where you can set up and customize settings for your own stream.

Using Active Sharing

Periodically, YouTube releases new features for the YouTube Web site. One of the more recent features (at least in the last year that this book was written) is the ability to see when other users are watching a particular video. If a user has the Active Sharing feature enabled for their account, whenever they view a video on YouTube, anyone else who is viewing that video at the same time (or up to a half-hour afterward on your channel page) will see the name of the user who is watching the video. The maximum number of names you can see at a time is 25. This is yet another way to get noticed on YouTube.

Follow these steps to turn on Active Sharing for your account:

1. Make sure you are logged on to your account, and then click My Account at the top of any YouTube page.

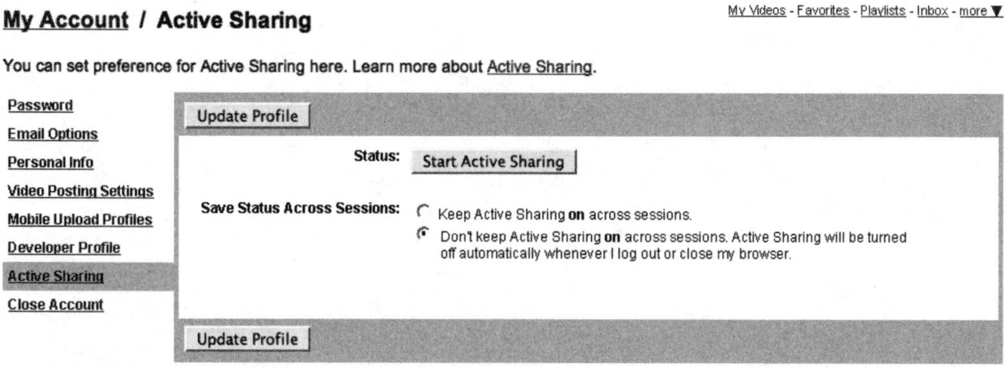

My Account / Active Sharing

You can set preference for Active Sharing here. Learn more about Active Sharing.

Password

Email Options

Personal Info

Video Posting Settings

Mobile Upload Profiles

Developer Profile

Active Sharing

Close Account

Update Profile

Status: Start Active Sharing

Save Status Across Sessions: ○ Keep Active Sharing **on** across sessions.

● Don't keep Active Sharing **on** across sessions. Active Sharing will be turned off automatically whenever I log out or close my browser.

Update Profile

FIGURE 5-24   When Active Sharing is turned on for a user, his or her account name appear next to the videos he or she is watching, which anyone who visits YouTube can see.

2. Look in the Account Settings section of your My Account page, and click the Active Sharing link.

3. On the Active Sharing page that appears, decide how you want to save your status across sessions for this feature (see Figure 5-24).

4. When you are ready, click the Start Active Sharing button.

NOTE   *You can also turn on Active Sharing by clicking the History link at the top of a page, clicking Active Sharing, and then clicking Start Active Sharing. This is also where you can view videos that you watched with Active Sharing turned on.*

In this chapter, you looked at many ways to interact with videos on YouTube, organize and manage your account, and participate in a variety of community features. In the next chapter, you'll expand on what you've learned by thinking about some ways to improve your profile and get noticed on YouTube.

Chapter 6

Customizing Your YouTube Channel and Using Special Tools

How to...

- Add more information to your channel
- Modify the design of your channel
- Use RSS feeds
- Experiment with YouTube APIs
- Download YouTube videos

Once you've become accustomed to viewing, uploading, and managing videos on YouTube, you can use additional tools, some of which YouTube provides, to customize your channel, making it more appealing to potential visitors. The customization process involves adding more information about your channel, as well as modifying the look of your channel by changing colors and adding images. In this chapter, you will learn how to customize your YouTube channel and explore some of the options for more advanced features.

Customizing Your YouTube Channel

You've been working with your YouTube account in previous chapters, using it to upload videos, manage your contacts, and even edit and enhance your videos. In this section, we discuss how to further customize and add style to your channel using a variety of options that YouTube provides.

Modifying Basic Channel Information

Each account has some basic channel information associated with it, such as the title and description of the channel, as well as options for leaving comments, displaying bulletins, and changing the channel type for your account (see Figure 6-1). The following steps discuss each of the options that are currently available to you:

1. Click the My Account link at the top of any YouTube page. If you are not already logged on to your account, you will be prompted to do so before proceeding.

2. Under the Channel Settings section of your My Account page, click Channel Info.

3. On the Edit Channel Info page that appears, you can enter a new title for your page if you desire, as well as a description, if you don't already have one. By adding a relevant title and description, YouTube users will be able to find you better in searches and you'll be able to communicate your message better.

4. In the Channel Icon area, select either Use The Last Video I Uploaded As My Profile Picture or I'll Select The Profile Picture From "My Videos." Most users will probably want to choose their profile picture manually (the small picture that appears next to the name of their channel wherever it appears), although using the last video you

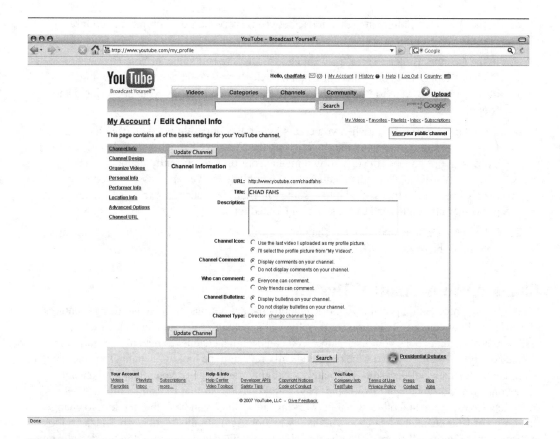

FIGURE 6-1 The Channel Information page of your account allows you to add or modify basic information.

uploaded may help to draw people to your newest videos. The second option is chosen automatically if you have already clicked the Make Channel Icon option for a particular video.

5. In the Channel Comments area, select either Display Comments On Your Channel or Do Not Display Comments On Your Channel, depending on whether or not you want others to see the comments that users have been leaving. Whether you choose this option or not probably depends on the nature of the comments that users have been leaving. If they are complimentary, then it reflects well on your channel. Also, comments are an important social aspect of YouTube, which helps to bring together viewers with common interests. While you may be at risk for an occasional negative comment, it's often a good idea to provide viewers with the opportunity to bond and to even dispute bad comments, which is only possible if you choose to display them.

6. In the Who Can Comment area, choose between Everyone Can Comment and Only Friends Can Comment.

7. In the Channel Bulletins area, you can choose Display Bulletins On Your Channel or Do Not Display Bulletins On Your Channel, which may again depend on how much information you want to be viewable by the general public or just your subscribers and friends.

8. The channel type was set when you created your account, although you can change it from its current type to any other by clicking the Change Channel Type link and selecting a different option from the drop-down menu. Your options currently include YouTuber, Director, Musician, Comedian, and Guru. The only negative repercussion to changing the channel type is that you will lose some information if changing from an account with performer info data, such as Musician or Comedian.

9. When you are done updating the channel information, click Update Channel at the top or bottom of the page.

Changing Your Channel Design

While channel information pertains to more general channel options, the channel design features of YouTube allow you to fully customize the physical appearance of your channel, which is visible to anyone that clicks your user name. You can design a channel to match your particular "brand" or style. You may also decide to periodically redesign the look of a channel to celebrate a holiday or other special occasion. Ultimately, changing the design of your channel makes it more your own and sets it apart from other pages on YouTube, similar to using templates on MySpace, LiveJournal, and other social networking sites. Since you have the freedom to change the design of your channel as much as you like, why not use it? In this section, you'll take a look at the variety of options that are currently available to anyone who is interested in the design and layout of their channel (see Figure 6-2).

Selecting a Theme and Changing Layout Properties

The following steps walk you through the process of modifying the most basic channel design options for your account:

1. If you're not already logged on to your account, click the My Account link at the top of any YouTube page.

2. Under the Channel Settings section of your My Account page, click Channel Design.

3. At the top of the Channel Design page, under the Select A Theme section, choose a basic color theme for your channel from the nine available themes that are listed. Clicking an option to select a color theme displays the results in the Channel Preview area of the page. Try a variety of options before settling on a theme. You can always come back at any time and choose a different set of colors to match your mood or to better represent the look and feel of your videos.

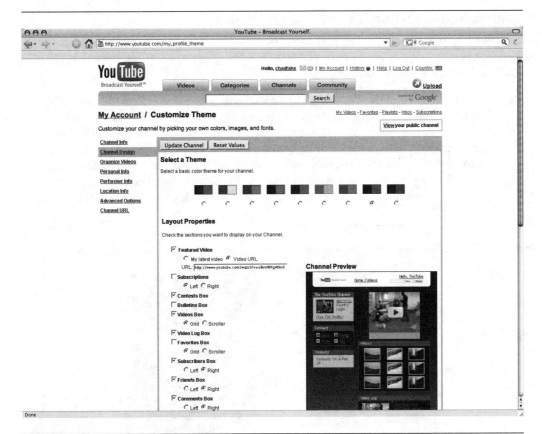

FIGURE 6-2 The channel design area of your account offers a wide range of options for customizing the look of your channel.

4. In the Layout Properties section of the page, select the check boxes for the areas that you want to display on your channel. By selecting Featured Video, you also have the choice of showing your latest video or the video Uniform Resource Locator (URL). Additional options include Subscriptions, Contests Box, Bulletins Box, Videos Box, Video Log Box, Favorites Box, Subscribers Box, Friends Box, and Comments Box. Note that some of these choices include the option to position the section on the left or right of the page or with a grid or scroller. Once again, you can preview the choices that you make by looking at the Channel Preview area on the right side of the page as you make your selections (the preview is in real time). The option to display certain sections and not others makes it possible to include only the most relevant information on your channel, eliminating empty boxes (for example, if you don't have subscribers or friends), limiting information that is viewable to the general public, and effectively alleviating clutter.

Advanced Design Customization and Properties

The following steps walk you through the process of modifying the advanced channel design options for your account (see Figure 6-3), which include the ability to select specific colors for your channel as well as background images:

1. On the bottom half of the Channel Design page, in the Advanced Design Customization area, select a specific background color by typing a precise hexadecimal code (a six-character code used to specify colors for the Web, such as #ffffff for white or #000000 for black, as discussed in the following section of this chapter), or by clicking the Pick link to the right of the field and choosing a color by sight, using the color swatches that appear. The Channel Preview area of the page should display the choices you have made, unless you currently have a background image selected, as described in the next step.

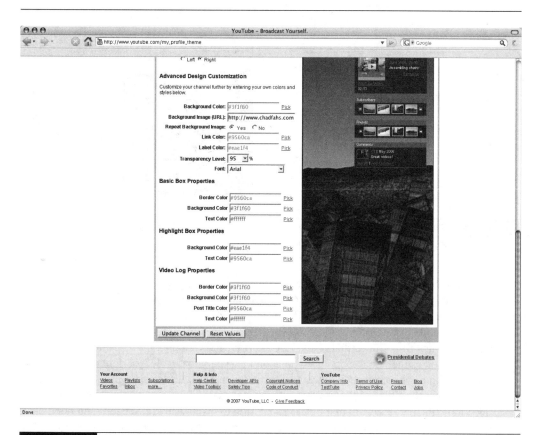

FIGURE 6-3   The advanced design customization options allow you to select specific colors and images for your channel.

2. If you'd rather use an image as your background instead of a solid color, enter the URL that points to the image (such as http://www.chadfahs.com/wallpaper/City_AD_1920.jpg) in the Background Image (URL) field. Currently, the image link that you use needs to be an external link to an image that is hosted on another site, which can be drawn from your own Web site, pulled from a favorite Web page, or stored on a site like Flickr. The only limitations are (potentially) copyright restrictions and size of the image. An image with a large file size will load too slowly, and an image with dimensions that exceed the average browser display may not look very good. Conversely, an image whose dimensions are too small may not fill out the page, which leads us to the next step.

3. In the Repeat Background Image area, choose Yes or No, depending on whether you want YouTube to tile the image or not. A small image should most likely be tiled, while a large photo may not. Often, an image that was not designed to be tiled can make a page appear chaotic and cluttered. Check the Channel Preview area to determine if this layout will work for your page. You can find a tutorial on tiling images at www.chadfahs.com.

4. If desired, you can also select a color value for the link color (any underlined hyperlinks on your channel page) and label color (such as the running time of your videos or the date that a comment was placed). Do this by entering a color value or using the Pick link to select a color swatch.

5. Next, you can choose a transparency level from the drop-down menu for all of the elements that float over the background. The default value is 95%, although you can set it anywhere from 50% to 100%.

6. Select the look of your text by choosing an option from the Font drop-down menu. The choice of font is always crucial to any design, although you are currently limited to Arial, Times New Roman, Georgia, or Verdana.

7. Under the Basic Box Properties section, you can select colors for the border color, the background color or the text color of all your boxes (the box that surrounds each of the areas on your channel, such as the box around Videos, Favorites, Subscribers, etc.).

8. Under the Highlight Box Properties section, you can select colors for the background color or text color of all your box properties (the interior of the box that surrounds each of the areas on your channel).

9. Under the Video Log Properties section, you can select colors for the border color, background color, post title color, or text color of items within the Video Log portion of your channel.

10. When you have double-checked the Channel Preview area and are satisfied with the new look of your channel, click the Update Channel button at the top or bottom of the Channel Design page. Your channel has now been updated with your new design!

Choosing Color Values for the Web

As you saw with the advanced design customization options for YouTube, precise color values can be set for the Web using a color system that is defined by a six-character code. These hexadecimal color values are based on a 256-color system, which ensures that the colors you choose look (more or less) the same, regardless of what computer they are viewed on, which means that they are considered "Web-safe." Of course, not all displays are calibrated correctly, but it's about as close as you will get to an exact match. By including these codes in the Hypertext Markup Language (HTML) or other coding language that defines the construction of a Web site, you can set the color of the text, background, tables, or other parts of a page that are interpreted by a Web browser. If you use software like Photoshop or Dreamweaver to design Web sites, you can easily sample and preview Web-safe colors that you want to use. If you see a color that you like online, in a photo, or somewhere else on your computer screen, you can sample it and then use its closest Web-safe color (defined by the corresponding hexadecimal code) to add to your Web site or your YouTube channel design. If you're on a Mac, you can use the included DigitalColor Meter application (see Figure 6-4), located in your Utilities folder. PC users can choose from any number of free applications available online (such as the one available at http://colorcop.net). In addition, if you are a Windows Vista user, you can use a Vista Gadget for making color selections and comparisons. By moving the eyedropper tool in these applications over a color that you like, you can see the hexadecimal code value, which can then be applied to your YouTube channel as described earlier.

If you are interested in selecting multiple color values to create a harmonious color scheme for your channel design, consider using Adobe's kuler Web site at http://kuler.adobe.com. Here you can find a large number of pleasing color palettes to match your needs or you can design one of your own. Although the color combinations listed here may be a bit too complex for your particular channel's design, they can get you started thinking about the many possible uses for color on a Web site, or in any other graphic design application for that matter.

Organizing Your Videos

The arrangement of videos on your channel can have a great effect on what gets seen (see Figure 6-5). In this section, you'll learn how to change the arrangement of your videos using the Organize Videos option of your account.

1. Click the My Account link at the top of any YouTube page. If you are not already logged on to your account, you will be prompted to do so before proceeding.

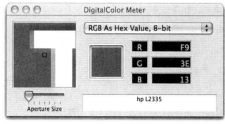

FIGURE 6-4   Sampling colors that you like is a good way to make satisfying color choices.

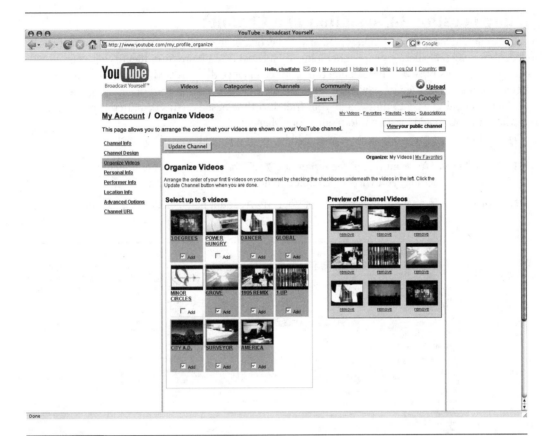

FIGURE 6-5 You can easily change the arrangement of videos on your channel, although you are currently limited to nine videos on a page.

2. Under the Channel Settings section of your My Account page, click Organize Videos.

3. On the Organize Videos page that appears, select the Add check box underneath the videos on the left that you want to appear first on your channel page. You can select up to nine videos. On the right side of the page, you can see how the videos you chose will appear grouped on the page. To remove a video that you have previously chosen to add, click the Remove link underneath one of the videos in the Preview Of Channel Videos area on the right.

4. When you are finished organizing your videos, click the Update Channel button at the top or bottom of the page.

Adding Location Information to a Channel

Another option in the Channel Settings area of your account is the ability to set location information so that users may see where you are geographically located (see Figure 6-6). Identifying your location for viewers provides more context for your channel (videos created in Texas may be different from those created in New York, for example). However (as a word of caution), it also makes it (potentially) easy to find you or your friends offline based on this data. In this procedure, you will learn how to add location information for a channel.

The following steps demonstrate how to add location information to a channel:

1. Click the My Account link at the top of any YouTube page. If you are not already logged on to your account, you will be prompted to do so before proceeding.

2. Under the Channel Settings section of your My Account page, click Location Info.

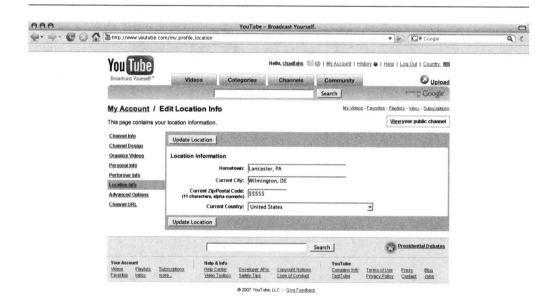

FIGURE 6-6 Location information can be added for your channel.

3. On the Edit Location Info page that appears, enter information for your hometown (where you were born or raised), current city, current ZIP/postal code, and current country from the relevant drop-down menus.

4. When you are done entering location information for your channel, click the Update Location button at the top or bottom of the page.

Modifying Advanced Options

Depending on the account type you have chosen, you may see an Advanced Options link on your My Account page (this is true with Director accounts, for example), which provides options for including a URL for another Web site (for example, if you have a blog or Web site of your own) and adding an icon graphic for your channel (see Figure 6-7). If you choose to create a special channel icon, you should create it in an application like Photoshop at dimensions of 55 × 55 pixels.

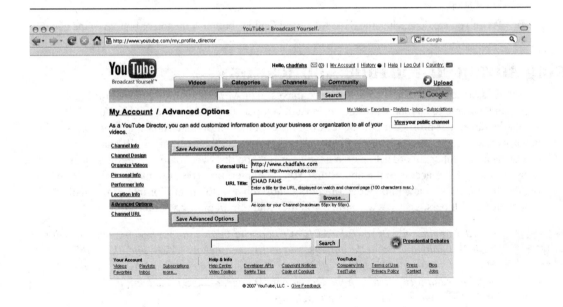

FIGURE 6-7   Advanced options for a channel include providing an external URL and choosing a channel icon.

The following steps demonstrate how to modify the advanced options for your channel:

1. Click the My Account link at the top of any YouTube page. If you are not already logged on to your account, you will be prompted to do so before proceeding.

2. Under the Channel Settings section of your My Account page, click Advanced Options.

3. On the Advanced Options page that appears, enter the external URL for a personal Web site (in the format of http://www.chadfahs.com), as well as a title that you want associated with it (such as Chad Fahs' Homepage).

4. Under the Channel Icon text box, click the Choose File button, and select an icon graphic on your computer's hard drive that you have created for use with your channel. As mentioned, the graphic should have square dimensions of 55 × 55 pixels in order to avoid any stretching. If you have an image that is not natively square, considering pasting it into a document with a solid color background and then correcting the proportions using Photoshop.

5. When you are done, click the Save Advanced Options button at the top or bottom of the page.

Using Advanced YouTube Applications

For more advanced Web developers, YouTube makes their API (application programming interface) available to anyone who signs up as a developer. To get started using YouTube APIs, fill out the developer profile and then check out the documentation that YouTube provides, which can answer some of the technical questions you might have. In this section, you'll learn how to sign up as a developer (in order to gain a developer ID) and discover some of the things you can do by gaining greater access to the underlying YouTube interface. The examples in this section assume that you have some knowledge of coding and Web development. For more information on tools for developers, visit www.youtube.com/dev and http://apiblog.youtube.com.

NOTE   *In order to make use of YouTube APIs, it's important that you first become familiar with basic Web languages that developers frequently use, such as HTML and eXtensible Markup Language (XML). You will also need to be familiar with at least one of the developer platforms listed on the Developer ID page, although the availability of some of the tools may be limited by your Web host.*

Getting a Developer ID

The first thing you need to do if you want to participate as a developer is get a Developer ID. To do this, you need to sign up as a developer on YouTube (see Figure 6-8). The following steps will demonstrate how to sign up as a developer from your current account:

1. Click the My Account link at the top of any YouTube page. If you are not already logged on to your account, you will be prompted to do so before proceeding.

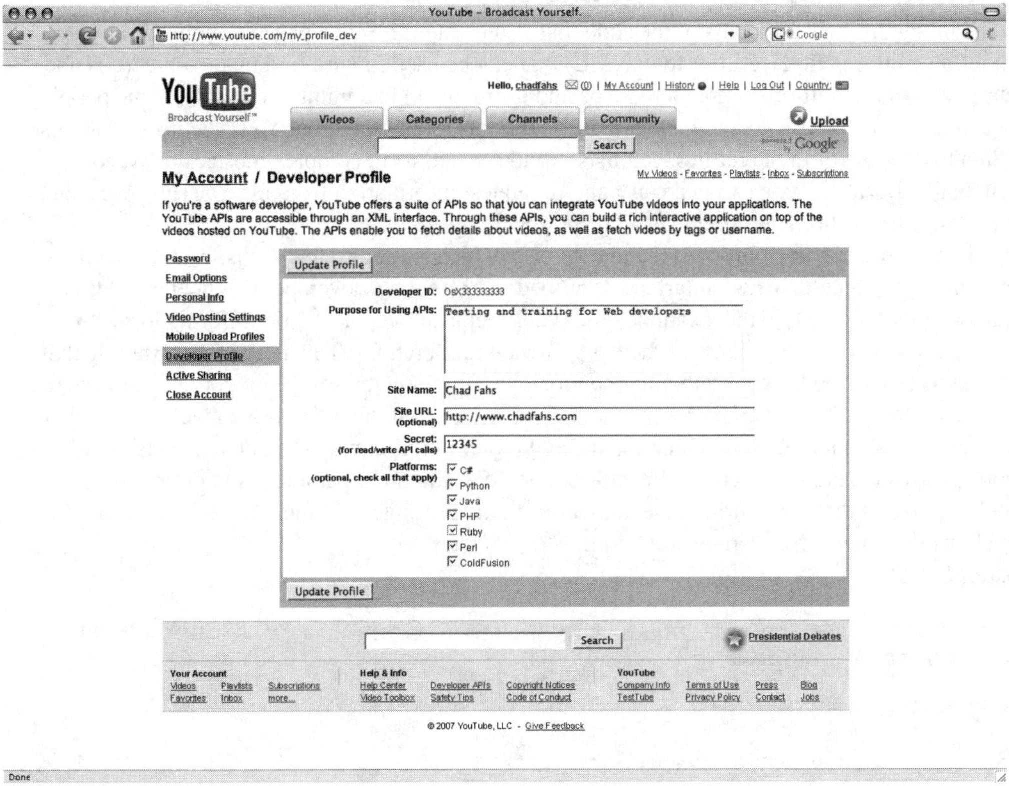

FIGURE 6-8   A Developer ID gives you access to YouTube's APIs.

2. Under the Account Settings section of your My Account page, click Developer Profile.

3. On the Developer Profile page that appears, fill out the fields, including Purpose For Using APIs, Site Name (your home page name or the Web site name you will likely use these features on), Site URL (an optional field that lists the URL to the page where these APIs may be used), Secret (another optional field where you will read/write API calls), and then select the check boxes for the platforms that you are developing for. Your choices include C#, Python, Java, PHP, Ruby, Perl, and Cold Fusion.

4. When you are finished filling out the profile, click Save Profile. Your newly created Developer ID is now listed at the top of the profile. This ID can be used in the APIs that you create.

Creating a Simple API Call and Response

By including different API calls in the code that you create for a Web page or application, you can retrieve information (results are in XML) that can be used to view and manipulate YouTube data (for example, information about videos and user names) in a number of ways. Some people have used YouTube APIs to augment Google Maps data (something that YouTube itself is almost certain to do more of in the future), call lists of videos, and form complex mosaics of video thumbnails. Basically, you can make a "call" to request information from the YouTube Web site, and if the call is valid, you should get a "response" in return.

The following is an example call and response, which is used to fetch a list of videos with a particular tag (using the REST interface described in YouTube's developer documents at http://youtube.com/dev_rest). In this example, you would replace the placeholder information with your Developer ID and the name of the tag you want to search for. This is a simple example that you can test in a Web browser, although you may need to view the source on your page to see the XML data. Notice in the sample results that information about the video is also included, such as its length, view count, number of comments, and more. In this example, I entered "cats" (without quotations) as the tag to search for. In addition, you can add more parameters to define the number of pages that are returned, the number of items per page, and more. Check out YouTube's developer documents for more information.

Example Call

```
http://www.youtube.com/api2_rest?method=youtube.videos.list_by_tag&dev_id=YOUR_
DEVELOPER_ID&tag=TAG_NAME
```

Example Response

```
<?xml version="1.0" encoding="utf-8"?>
<ut_response status="ok">
<total>220847</total>
<video_list>
<video>
<author>neverende</author>
<id>pIqhUCZgwXQ</id>
<title>funny cats</title>
<length_seconds>98</length_seconds>
<rating_avg>4.82</rating_avg>
<rating_count>19401</rating_count>
<description>funny cats</description>
<view_count>10678042</view_count>
<upload_time>1135084749</upload_time>
<comment_count>8177</comment_count>
<tags>cats funny</tags>
<url>http://www.youtube.com/?v=pIqhUCZgwXQ</url>
<thumbnail_url>http://img.youtube.com/vi/pIqhUCZgwXQ/default.jpg</thumbnail_url>
</video>
</video_list>
```

Accessing YouTube RSS Feeds

RSS (Really Simple Syndication) is utilized by many blogs and Web sites to publish content using a document called a feed. An RSS feed usually contains a summary of text from a participating Web site, particularly news, podcasts, or other information that is updated often. For most users, the main advantage of RSS feeds is that they save time having to visit several Web sites to check on the latest posts or news items. With RSS, the news comes to you. In the case of YouTube, you can use RSS feeds to access videos and deliver them to your Web site or browser without needing to visit the site yourself or conduct searches in the usual manner. By creating a simple RSS feed of a YouTube search, you can instantly retrieve the latest results. For more information on YouTube's RSS feeds, including several examples of feeds that you might use, visit www.youtube.com/rssls.

The following code can be typed into your browser's address bar to test out the RSS feature, replacing the tag name with a tag you want to search for ("cats," for example):

```
http://www.youtube.com/rss/tag/TAG NAME.rss
```

Alternately, you can type the following to establish a feed:

```
feed://www.youtube.com/rss/tag/TAG NAME.rss
```

If you wanted to create a feed for a particular YouTube user's channel, you could enter the following (replacing "insert username" with a real channel, such as chadfahs):

```
feed://www.youtube.com/rss/user/INSERT_USERNAME/videos.rss
```

Assuming that you are using a newer browser, like Firefox or Safari, it will have an RSS reader built in that formats the results for you (see Figure 6-9). Other dedicated RSS readers and RSS aggregators are available as well, such as NetNewsWire, FeedReader, and many more.

Downloading YouTube Videos

Although YouTube does not officially support or condone the downloading of videos, it is possible to extract video from the site and play it back using a special FLV (Flash Video) player. This can be accomplished by using free applications found online or by using special Web sites that will download the video for you. In this section, you will see a few ways that YouTube videos may be downloaded. However, for legal purposes, it's a good idea to check out the site's terms of service at www.youtube.com/t/terms, which states (among other stipulations) that videos can only be accessed for streaming. According to YouTube, " 'Streaming' means a contemporaneous digital transmission of an audiovisual work via the Internet from the YouTube Service to a user's device in such a manner that the data is intended for real-time viewing and not intended to be copied, stored, permanently downloaded, or redistributed by the user.

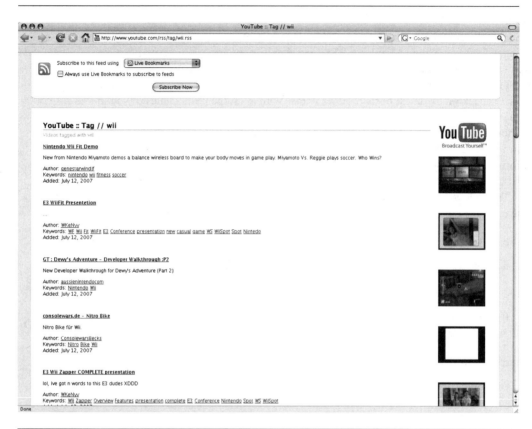

FIGURE 6-9 RSS feeds are a convenient way to access news or data on a Web site that frequently changes.

Accessing User Videos for any purpose or in any manner other than Streaming is expressly prohibited. User Videos are made available 'as is.' "

There are a variety of Web sites that will help you to download videos from YouTube. One such site is www.keepvid.com. By visiting this site, pasting the YouTube URL to the desired video in the box at the top of the page, selecting YouTube from the drop-down menu, and clicking the Submit button, you are presented with a link to download the file. Similar sites include Video Downloader (with optional Firefox extension) at http://javimoya.com/blog/youtube_en.php, www.saveyoutube.com, www.youtubex.com, and many more, most of which are similar in functionality.

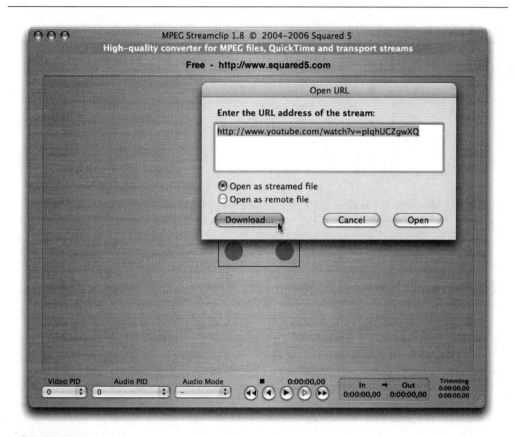

FIGURE 6-10 Applications like MPEG Streamclip allow you to download YouTube videos.

In addition to using a Web site to download YouTube videos, there are some free software applications available that include the ability to grab videos from YouTube. One such application is called MPEG Streamclip (www.squared5.com) for Mac and Windows, which is also an excellent media player (although currently not for FLVs) and converter for other media files (see Figure 6-10). Additional software for downloading YouTube videos includes YouRipper (www.remlapsoftware.com), and others that can be found online.

Chapter 7

Promoting Your Videos on YouTube

How to...

- Improve your chances of success on YouTube
- Familiarize yourself with online video promotion
- Include relevant information for your videos and YouTube channel
- Add videos to a Web page or blog
- Understand the processes used by successful video creators

Creating an account, uploading videos, and generally participating in the YouTube community is great, but getting your videos seen by a large number of people is the only way to achieve YouTube fame (and possibly fortune). One of the most popular ways to get your videos seen is by adding them (or a link) to a Web page outside of YouTube. Of course, it's also essential to add the appropriate information to your videos if you want people to find them on their own. Generating "buzz" is also important, which can be done by getting press or other users to review your videos.

In fact, there are a number of ways in which you can improve your viewership and expand your video presence online, whether YouTube is the final destination or just the beginning. YouTube and other social networking sites are a great way to hook potential audience members and customers before sending them to your own Web site or to one of the other online video sites that pays for popular videos.

In this chapter, you will learn about these and several other strategies for promoting your videos on YouTube. At the end of the chapter, successful YouTube personalities and video creators will add their voices to the discussion on what it takes to get noticed.

Viral Video

A discussion of online video promotion would not be complete without first acknowledging a phenomenon known as the "viral video." Basically, viral videos are what the name (and its biological roots) implies. These videos gain popularity rapidly through transmission from one user to the next, often through e-mail or posting on a Web site or blog. The qualities of a viral video frequently include elements of humor, a timely subject matter, and exuberant inventiveness, such as a unique concept that acts as the hook to draw viewers in. Producing a video that becomes a viral hit is the dream of many a YouTuber. As a result of their wide footprint and verifiable appeal, viral videos are also popular among marketers promoting a variety of products and movies. One of the biggest viral video hits from recent memory is the "Extreme Diet Coke and Mentos experiment," which scored several million views (see Figure 7-1). Another example is the "Lazy Sunday" sketch that played on *Saturday Night Live*. Amateur videos like the "Star Wars Kid" and the "Numa Numa" song were equally popular, as was the "Here It Goes Again" music video for the band OK Go. In fact, the actual definition of viral video encompasses any video whose popularity spreads widely through sharing on the Internet.

FIGURE 7-1   A viral video's popularity spreads quickly, usually due to its humor and surprising concept, such as the "Extreme Diet Coke and Mentos Experiment."

Achieving Popularity on YouTube

While there is no guaranteed method for achieving popularity on YouTube, there are many things you can do to increase your chances of success. The following list represents the most common approaches that can be used for virtually any video created for YouTube.

- **Improve your production quality**   While most successful YouTube videos are not exactly ready for prime time, they are a bit more polished than the glut of "amateur" content on YouTube. As always, there are exceptions, particularly with viral videos that become popular as the result of an outrageous stunt or a newsworthy event caught on a camera phone. Perhaps your results could be improved by using more creative camera work and editing (such as additional angles and a faster pace). Careful framing and attention to lighting can go a long way as well, even for video blogs or videos with only a couple of setups. Audio quality is also important, which can be improved through the placement of a microphone and the removal of background noise. In any case, thinking about how you put something on video can be just as important as what you choose to record. Viewers are more likely to stick with something that is not painful to their eyes and ears. Don't worry about making your pieces look too polished, since without the budgets of a Hollywood studio, there's little chance that someone will mistake your video with the latest Bruckheimer epic. In general, showing your viewers that you have a handle on your craft inspires confidence in your abilities as a storyteller, demonstrates respect for your audience, and gives them the feeling that they are not wasting their time.

■ **Add more visual appeal**   The other side to production quality is the talent, props, and sets that you choose to include in your videos. When selecting a location to record your video, choose appealing environments, even if it means rearranging a bedroom or office to create a pleasing "set" design. Visual appeal can also come in the form of extra graphic elements (carefully designed titles or animations) and special effects, which temporarily elevate a typical YouTube video to more a design-conscious level. Any additional elements that you can think of to hook potential viewers with their eyes (particularly in the still image that is associated with each video) increase your chance of success. Visual appeal may even be added to webcam videos by varying facial expressions and moving your head around a bit instead of staring directly into the camera without blinking for prolonged periods. Similarly, aural appeal can be added by reading your script or delivering your blog entry with enough inflection and emotion, while avoiding a monotone delivery.

■ **Fill a niche**   There are countless areas of special interest that are represented on YouTube. Knowing which one of these groups (or range of interests) that you want to target is critical to getting your message across, even if that message is simply to visit your channel and watch more of your videos. An understanding of your target market and its makeup will guide many of the choices that you make, starting with production considerations, and ending with where you will place your videos to achieve optimal exposure. If you're looking to break into YouTube, finding an area that hasn't been sufficiently covered might be one approach. Many successful companies (YouTube included) got where they are by filling a need that was, as yet, unsuccessfully fulfilled. Finding a niche and filling it with videos that are produced well and that meet the requirements of its potential viewers is one starting point for success.

■ **Make it timely**   Reading the pulse of other YouTube users or the community at large can be difficult. It requires research or a natural intuition about trends and, in the end, is often a matter of luck. Still, it may be the key to finding a formula (if there is such as thing) for YouTube success. Alternately, documenting important events means putting yourself in the right place at the right time, which can be an equally elusive proposition. You can begin to stay acquainted with what's happening in a particular community by reading a lot of blogs, fishing around for information in discussion groups or through e-mail lists, polling your friends or colleagues about their interests, and simply doing your "homework" when it comes to an area that seems interesting.

■ **Make your videos easy to find**   Without providing relevant data about your videos, it will be difficult for users to locate them. Even users who are interested in the subjects covered by your videos will have a hard time if they have not been properly described and tagged. Begin by adding a description that includes as many specific details as possible. Adding relevant tags may also be useful, so consider what keywords users are likely to use in a search.

■ **Build a network**   It's easy to promote your video if you already have a network of interested viewers in place. Once someone subscribes to your channel, you've got an instant audience every time you upload a new video. Of course, it's not so easy to gain subscribers. Once you've had some success with one or more videos (perhaps even a viral video hit), then you can more easily build a solid subscriber base—on rare occasions, this may happen overnight.

- **Seed your videos online** Post links to your videos or embed the video into blogs, discussion groups, and other Web pages like MySpace as much as you can. Try to get your videos reviewed by sites online, such as popular blogs. Post comments to other videos on YouTube or similar social networking sites, along with a link to your video. If your video fits well into a particular niche, then make sure to get visibility on any sites or community groups that are related to that area of interest.

Understanding Online Video Promotion

Now that you have an idea of what is required in many cases to increase the likelihood that your video gets seen, it's also important to think more critically about the process of online video promotion in general. In fact, it's important to consider some of the principles that make online video an attractive method for promotion in the first place. Why should a filmmaker, for example, post his or her video on a site like YouTube, and what kinds of results should be expected? What are the methods used by professional marketers, and how can you make them work for your independent video projects?

The world of online video promotion can be a noisy marketplace, full of both original content and not-so-appealing commercial advertisements. Ultimately, the goal is to get exposure and achieve fame, sell a product, or both. Large corporations, movie studios, retailers, and small business owners use YouTube everyday for this purpose. However, it's important to be realistic about what to expect. YouTube is not always the best, or only, outlet for your video. For example, YouTube is not currently a realistic choice for showing full-length movies, even though there have been a few notable exceptions, although this may change in the future. As mentioned, it's also a noisy marketplace, overflowing with a wide variety of products and ideas, and it's easy to get lost in the millions of videos that are uploaded on a regular basis. There are no guarantees for success, even for well-thought out marketing campaigns. What's popular one day is no longer fashionable the next.

The quality of YouTube's encoded video also plays a role in the types of products that may be successfully promoted on the site. What looks good on a DVD, or even as a podcast for iTunes, may fall apart visually when uploaded to YouTube. Knowing how to work within YouTube's limitations is important, particularly at this early stage of its development. If you're promoting a product that looks good on a high-definition television (HDTV), for example, you might want to think about creative ways to get that across in a video that is specifically designed for YouTube. Perhaps that means creating a promotional video that's really a teaser and that does not include footage from your original program. If you're promoting a film, why not upload behind-the-scenes footage instead? You might even try staging a publicity stunt to draw attention in an unusual way, much like David Lynch did by sitting on the corner of a busy intersection in Los Angeles along with a real cow and a poster advertising his movie *Inland Empire*. After all, thinking outside of the box (the "box" being traditional TV and movie theaters) is what online video is all about.

For another perspective on the topic of using YouTube as an outlet for presenting and promoting videos (particularly for aspiring filmmakers), I spoke to Scott Kirsner, author of the book *The Future of Web Video* and editor of the blog "CinemaTech" (http://cinematech.blogspot .com), which covers digital entertainment. According to Scott.

"In the early days of YouTube (2005 and 2006, basically), a lot of filmmakers looked at the site and dismissed it. Users were watching short-form videos, not 90-minute movies, and the quality wasn't anywhere close to what you'd get on a DVD, let alone on the big screen of a multiplex. But as YouTube's audience grew so rapidly, I think filmmakers and movie studios started to realize that this wasn't a phenomenon you could ignore.

"Most have decided to try using YouTube to promote their movies with excerpts, trailers, behind-the-scenes footage, and snippets. When *Scary Movie 4* came out in April 2006, the marketing agency Deep Focus paid for placement on YouTube's home page to attract viewers to the trailer. Since then, it has been seen more than six million times. (It doesn't hurt that the still-frame image for the clip shows a woman taking a shower—always a good way to arouse viewers' interest.)

"Other filmmakers, like San Jose-based animator M dot Strange, have used YouTube in a more organic way. He has posted videos about how he makes his movies, his experiences at the Sundance Film Festival, and advice for other filmmakers. YouTube's editors have occasionally featured him for free on the home page. And by virtue of all the attention his work received on YouTube, he has been covered in mainstream publications like *The New York Times*. But I think getting in touch with YouTube's editors or getting their attention by virtue of something you've made is a giant challenge.

"Clearly, there's a big opportunity on YouTube in posting clips from a full-length movie and then trying to drive viewers to your Web site, where they can find out where the movie is playing or buy a DVD or digital download.

"But it's still not obvious whether YouTube wants to distribute full-length movies. They limit uploads to 100 megabytes (interestingly, Google Video doesn't have a length limit.) And they've only done one experiment, in June 2007, with making a full-length feature available: the indie movie *Four Eyed Monsters*. The business model there wasn't sharing any advertising revenue with the filmmakers (as YouTube has started to do in 2007 with some content partners), but rather allowing the filmmakers to have their own underwriter (the film site Spout.com) that provided them with income directly.

"I'm not convinced that YouTube is going to develop into a marketplace for hour-long content or full-length films—but it is already a powerful promotional engine for filmmakers willing to experiment."

Providing More Information about Your Channel and Videos

Although it might seem like a rudimentary idea, providing the right information about your videos is the key to getting them found by users who perform searches on YouTube, or even in search engines like Google. Once you've created your video and uploaded it, as described in previous chapters, it's time to think more carefully about how to improve the quality of information that you provide. For example, choosing the right account type (such as Guru or Musician) can be important, just as including location information can be useful for someone looking for videos created near their hometown or in a country on the other side of the world. Since you may never know for certain how people will find your videos, it's best to include as much information as possible to increase your odds of exposure.

Changing Personal and Performer Information

The personal and performer information that you provided when you set up your account may change, or you may wish to add more details that you left blank when you first started using YouTube. The more details you include, the better viewers will get to know you, your background, and your interests. As a result, more people may find your videos, or (in the case of performer information) may be redirected to other sites, where they can purchase your music, see your shows, and maybe even make you some money. In fact, if you are a performer (such as a musician or comedian), YouTube provides a special area of your account for more information about upcoming shows and album sales. In this section, you will learn how to update the personal and performer information to better promote your videos and services on YouTube.

Updating Personal Information

If you've used sites like MySpace before, then the type of personal information you can add to your YouTube channel will come as no surprise. Although, as with MySpace, you might want to exercise caution when revealing personal details about your life, both from a professional and safety point of view.

The following steps demonstrate how to edit and update your personal information:

1. Click the My Account link at the top of any YouTube page. If you are not already logged on to your account, you will be prompted to do so before proceeding.

2. Under the Channel Settings section of your My Account page, click Personal Info.

3. At this point, you can add or change any personal information that you want, such as your relationship status, age, a general description about yourself, the URL for your Web site (if you have one), and, of course, your name and gender. In addition, you can enter more information in the Professional Information section of the page, such as your occupations and company. Under the Student Information section, you can provide names of schools you have attended or currently attend. You can sometimes attract viewers with personal details that relate to their own, such as people who have attended the same school. Providing information about your occupation and companies might even get you additional work, if potential clients and employers like what they see.

4. Under the Interests section, enter information about your interests and hobbies, favorite movies and shows, favorite music, and favorite books, with each item in the corresponding text box separated by a comma.

5. When you are finished updating your personal information, click the Update Channel button at the top or bottom of the page.

Adding Performer Information and Event Dates

YouTube provides a great place to promote your band or variety act through the posting of videos, bulletins, and comments. The performer information that you add can provide additional details about where to see you on stage or where to find your music for sale. In addition, the information that you provide can help viewers with a particular musical, aesthetic, or comedic interest find you better (see Figure 7-2). If you have a YouTuber account, you won't have this option.

The following steps demonstrate how to edit and update your performer information:

1. Click the My Account link at the top of any YouTube page. If you are not already logged on to your account, you will be prompted to do so before proceeding.

2. Under the Channel Settings section of your My Account page, click Performer Info. Depending on the account type that you have chosen (such as YouTuber, Director, Musician, or Guru), you may or may not see certain details displayed here. As mentioned,

FIGURE 7-2   Performer information is available for every account type, except for YouTuber accounts.

if you have a YouTuber account, you won't even see the option to provide performer information displayed in your account. For all other accounts, the available details you can enter are different, as discussed later in this section.

3. Enter pertinent details for your particular account type, such as information you in general, your style, your influences, or other performers you are similar to.

4. When you are finished adding performer information, click the Update Channel button at the top or bottom of the page. If you have a Musician or Comedian account, proceed to the next step to add event dates.

As mentioned in the preceding steps, the performer information that you can provide differs according to the account type selected. These details can be useful in promoting your act through YouTube, and may even draw viewers to your videos as well. The options for each account type include the following:

- **Director**   About Me, Style (Acting, Art, Biography, Broadcaster, Commentary, Dance, Fashion, Model, News, Reviews, Talk Show, Variety, Vlogging), Influences, and Similar To

- **Musician**   About The Band, Style (A Cappella, Acoustic, Alt Country, Alternative, Americana, Art Rock, Bluegrass, Blues, Brit Pop, Celtic, Christian, Christian Rap, Christian Rock, Classical, Country, Crunk, Dance, Disco, Electronica, Electropop, Emo, Experimental, Folk, Folk-Rock, Freestyle, Funk, Garage Rock, Glam, Gospel, Goth, Grunge, Hard Rock, Hip-Hop, House, Indie Rock, Industrial, Jam Rock, Jazz, Jungle, Latin, Latin Pop, Mariachi, Metal, Miscellaneous, Motown, Old School Rap, Pop, Power Pop, Progressive Rock, Psychedelic, Psychobilly, Punk, Rap, R&B, Reggae, Retro, Rock, Rockabilly, Roots, Salsa, Singer–Songwriter, Ska, Soul, Southern Rap, Spoken Word, String Bands, Surf, Tango, Techno, Trance, Trip Hop Turntablist, World), Members, Formation Date, Record Label, Label Type (Independent, Major Label, Unsigned), Influences, and Sounds Like

- **Comedian**   About My Comedy, Comedy Style (Asian, Black, Blue Collar, Celebrity Humor, Clown, Gay/Lesbian, Hypnotist, Impersonations, Improv, Latino, Magic, Musical, Parody, Political, Sketch, Stand-Up), Influences, and Similar To

- **Guru**   About Me, Style (Beauty, Crafting, Educational, Financial, Fitness, Food + Drink, Home + Garden, Mechanics, Music, Relationship, Spiritual, Travel, Video), Influences, and Similar To

5. At this point, you may also add information for event dates on the Add A Show page (if you have a Musician or Comedian account) by clicking the Event Dates link on the left side of the screen. Options include fields for Show Date, Show Time, Venue, Address, City, ZIP/Postal Code, Country, Description, and Tickets URL.

6. When you are finished updating your event date information on the Add A Show page, click the Add Show button at the top or bottom of the page.

Changing Your Video Still

As you've seen countless times, each instance of a video on YouTube (when not visible in its own player window) is represented by a video still (also called a thumbnail or profile icon). Along with any corresponding text and descriptions, these stills are crucial for YouTube visitors to decide whether they want to watch your video. Whether it's on the YouTube Web site or embedded on an external site, the still that you choose for a video is an important part of the promotion process. Unfortunately, YouTube currently does not allow you to choose the exact frame you may want to represent your video. Instead, YouTube automatically selects the frame that occurs at the exact middle point of your video file. However, it is possible to choose from two other points in your video to select a still. At present, these points are one-quarter of the way from the beginning of your video and one-quarter of the way from the end of your video. In other words, the three possible stills that you can choose from are located at the one-quarter, one-half, and three-quarter points in your video (see Figure 7-3). If you are truly concerned about using a precise image for your thumbnail, you may even choose to plan your shots accordingly (or edit in an extra frame) so that the desired still image occurs at one of these moments in your video.

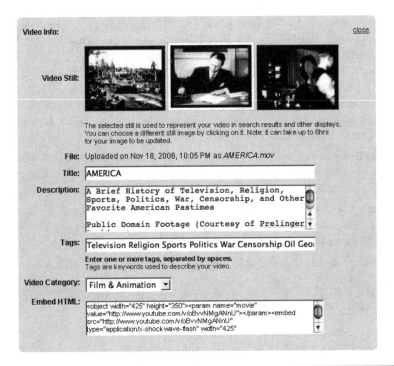

FIGURE 7-3   YouTube allows you to choose from three different preselected stills for each of the videos you have already uploaded to your account.

Follow these steps to select from three possible video still options for a particular video in your account:

1. Click the My Account link at the top of any YouTube page. If you are not already logged on to your account, you will be prompted to do so before proceeding.

2. Under the Videos section of your My Account page, click My Videos.

3. On the My Videos page that appears, click the Edit Video Info button next to a particular video.

4. On the Edit My Video page that appears, under the Video Info section, click the image that you want to use for the video still. Choose a frame that most accurately (or persuasively) represents your video.

5. When you are finished selecting the appropriate still for this video, click the Update Video Info button at the bottom of the page.

Adding Location Information to a Video

Since its acquisition by Google, YouTube has seen many changes. One of the changes is the ability to tag each video you create with information about where and when it was created (see Figure 7-4). In this way, each video is virtually mapped using a Google Maplet, providing another means for users to eventually find and identify pertinent videos.

The following steps demonstrate how to add location information to a video:

1. Click the My Account link at the top of any YouTube page. If you are not already logged on to your account, you will be prompted to do so before proceeding.

2. Under the Videos section of your My Account page, click My Videos.

3. On the My Videos page that appears, click the Edit Video Info button next to a particular video.

4. Towards the bottom of the Edit My Video page for this particular video, click the Choose Options link to the right of the Date And Map Options section. As soon as you click the link, additional options appear in this section of the page.

5. Choose the appropriate month, day, and year from the Date Recorded drop-down menu, or click Today if the video was just recorded.

6. Type a city location into the Map Video text field (such as Philadelphia, PA), and click the Search button to set that location.

7. Use the plus (+) and minus (–) buttons to zoom in or out until you find the precise location your video was shot, and then drag the marker in the map area to mark the location visually.

8. When you are finished setting location information for this video, click the Update Video Info button at the bottom of the page.

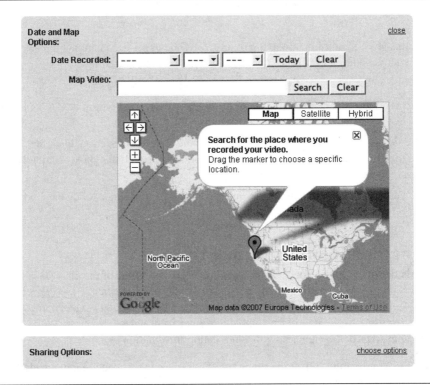

FIGURE 7-4   YouTube's relationship with Google has expanded with the introduction of Google's mapping features.

Directing Viewers to Your Videos

Once your videos are uploaded, you can use a variety of methods provided by YouTube to make them accessible on other Web pages and blogs, where they might be found by people that wouldn't otherwise find them on YouTube. In virtually all instances (except where only a link is provided), videos are embedded in a page by adding the corresponding Hypertext Markup Language (HTML) code generated by YouTube, which may also be modified by a user.

Embedding YouTube Videos on a Web Page

As mentioned, one of the best ways to get your videos seen is to embed them in another Web page. This page could be a blog (often a good place to advertise your video and get it seen) or your own Web site. Really, almost any place that you can add HTML to a page will allow you to embed a YouTube video (see Figure 7-5). Hopefully, visitors to these sites will choose to play your video, since it is conveniently placed and accessible without having to leave the current

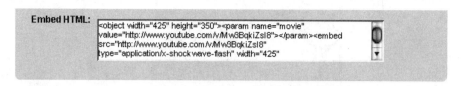

FIGURE 7-5   You can copy and paste the code for any video and embed it in your own Web page or blog.

page—no YouTube visit is required. Of course, it's great if a viewer becomes interested in your video and seeks out more work on your YouTube channel.

Embedding Videos with the New Player

YouTube makes embedding your videos easy by providing you with the code that you need. On each page for a particular video, YouTube includes an Embed section. Simply copy and paste this code into the HTML for your own Web site or blog, and the video will show up in a player window where you have added the code on that page.

The following is an example of the code provided by YouTube (with a sample link to a video). Your code will look slightly different, although it will likely be formatted in a similar way:

```
<object width="425" height="350"><param name="movie" value="http://
www.youtube.com/v/oBvvNMgANnU"></param><param name="wmode"
value="transparent"></param><embed src="http://www.youtube.com/v/
oBvvNMgANnU" type="application/x-shockwave-flash" wmode="transparent"
width="425" height="350"></embed></object>
```

Embedding Videos without the New Player Features

As you may have noticed, the new embedded video player is slightly different from the one that appears on the YouTube site for the same video (and is different from the old embedded player). The main difference is that embedded players now include special pop-up menus and options for watching related videos, along with the ability to quickly copy a link to the video or to grab the code so viewers can embed it on their own sites (see Figure 7-6). This is intended as a way to make related YouTube videos accessible remotely from another Web site and to add functionality that was previously available solely through the original YouTube page for the video. However, some users find the features of this new embedded player annoying and intrusive, particularly when you want to embed these videos on your own Web page and you don't have control over what videos YouTube will recommend.

If you want to remove the option to see related videos through the new embedded player, you can do so by clicking the Customize This Embed link next to the Embed field for a video, and then choose either Include Related Videos (this is selected by default and includes the new player features) or Don't Include Related Videos (the new player features are disabled). In addition, you

FIGURE 7-6   The features of YouTube's new player allow viewers to see related videos when a video is finished playing, although you can disable this feature if you wish.

can manually modify the code to remove the new features, making it look similar to the example listed below, which just adds "&rel=0" after the video ID number in the embed code (all other code remains the same for your video):

```
<object width="425" height="350"><param name="movie" value="http://
www.youtube.com/v/xxxxxx&rel=0" ></param><param name="wmode"
value="transparent"></param><embed src=" http://www.youtube.com/v/
xxxxxx&rel=0" type="application/x-shockwave-flash" wmode="transparent"
width="425" height="350"></embed></object>
```

Resizing an Embedded Video

If you look closely at the code generated by YouTube for embedded videos, you should see values listed for object width and height at the beginning of the code (basic experience with languages for the Web, such as HTML, are useful in this case). Curiously, since you have access to the code, you can easily resize the video to whatever dimensions that you want for your page, rather than using the default value of 425 × 350 pixels. For example, you can play the video at its native resolution of 320 × 240 pixels by entering those values for width and height, or expand it to play in a much larger window by entering values like 640 × 480 pixels. However, the quality of your embedded video doesn't improve when you make it larger. It might appear a little nicer when you make it smaller, in fact, since YouTube's additional stretching is not applied. For fun, you might even try making a very small video, such as 160 × 120 pixels, to see what your video looks like when it's formatted for a tight space.

Creating Custom Players

A recent addition to YouTube is the ability to customize the look of the player window for your embedded videos. Using this new feature, you can create more attractive designs for your embedded players (including color and layout) that fit the style of a particular page and (hopefully) will catch the eye of design-aware viewers (see Figure 7-7). It also allows you to include playlists of videos that are readily accessible to a user.

The following steps demonstrate how to create a custom embedded player for a YouTube video or playlist:

1. Click the My Account link at the top of any YouTube page. If you are not already logged on to your account, you will be prompted to do so before proceeding.

2. Under the Custom Players section of your My Account page, click the Create Custom Player button.

3. On the New Custom Player page that appears, start by adding player information, such as Player Name and Description.

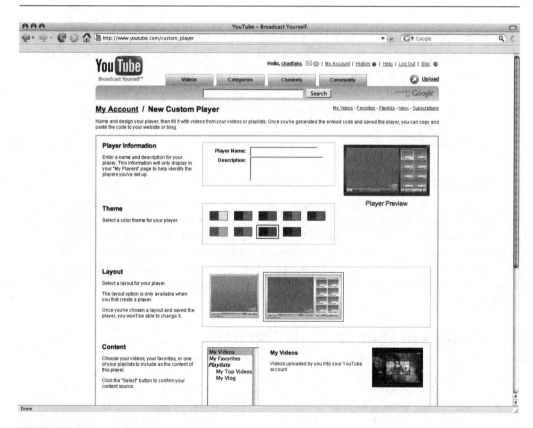

| FIGURE 7-7 | YouTube's custom video player adds colors and layouts not available in the standard player. |

4. Next, choose a color theme for your player by clicking one of the available color combinations. This option is similar to the color themes that you can create for your channel design. The current selection is also displayed in the Player Preview section of the page, which gives you an idea of what the player will look like when you're finished.

5. Next, choose whether you want a player for only one video or a layout that is designed to hold multiple video selections with a playlist by clicking the appropriate option.

6. On the Edit My Video page that appears, under the Video Info section, click the image that you want to use for the video still. The default selection is the middle point in your video, although you may choose frames that occur earlier or later in your video instead. Choose a frame that most accurately (or persuasively) represents your video.

7. Under the Content section on the New Custom Player page, choose My Videos, My Favorites, or a particular playlist, and then click the Select button to choose the source of content for the player.

8. When you are done customizing your new video player, click the Generate Code button in the Generate Code And Save Player section of the page.

9. Copy the code that appears in the Embed Code area, which can be pasted into a Web site to embed this player, just as you have done with the ordinary embed code previously discussed.

10. When you are done, click the Finish button at the bottom of the page, which brings you back to the My Custom Players page, where you can edit, remove, or create additional custom players.

Sending Links to Videos

Since each video on YouTube has its own unique link, it's easy to copy and paste that link into an e-mail that you can send to friends, post on a forum, or otherwise circulate throughout the "tubes" that connect people on the Internet. You can find the Uniform Resource Locator (URL) for a video on its main page. Simply copy and paste the URL that appears in your browser's address field into an e-mail or forum. It's as simple as that. You can also use the Share link underneath a video to send a URL that is formatted for a particular service like Digg, del.icio.us, Furl, and more.

Adding a Blog to Your YouTube Account

Many people have a blog where they can post their thoughts on topics ranging from the personal to the professional. In fact, much of the online "news" today is generated by blogs, or is at least commented on by them. YouTube users who have a blog can easily post videos directly to it using the video posting settings for their account. Currently, YouTube supports blogs created with Blogger, BlogSpot, WordPress, LiveJournal, Friendster, and Piczo (see Figure 7-8). If you don't have a blog, you can start one easily. In fact, they are a great place to promote your video! In this section, you will learn how to post video directly to a blog.

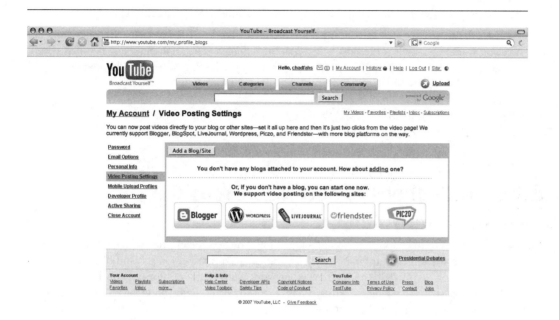

You can add a blog to your YouTube account, which includes support for BlogSpot, WordPress, LiveJournal, Friendster, and Piczo.

The following steps demonstrate how to add a blog to your YouTube account:

1. Click the My Account link at the top of any YouTube page. If you are not already logged on to your account, you will be prompted to do so before proceeding.

2. Under the Account Settings section of your My Account page, click Video Posting Settings.

3. On the Video Posting Settings page that appears, click the Add A Blog/Site button.

4. On the Add a Blog/Site page that appears, select the blog service that you use from the drop-down menu, and enter your user name and password for that blog. If you selected Friendster, you will need to enter an e-mail address and password instead. Self-hosted users of WordPress will need to enter an application programming interface (API) URL and API key, which were provided when you signed up for WordPress.

5. When you are finished adding a blog to your YouTube account, click Add Blog.

6. In order to post a video to your blog, simply locate the YouTube page for the video that you want to post, click the Post Video link that appears beneath it, enter any text that you want to include along with the video on your blog (including a title and additional text), and click the Post Video button to complete the operation.

> **NOTE** *You can find your WordPress API key by logging on to your WordPress account and clicking either Profile or My Account. A string of 12 letters and numbers will be listed on this page where it says "Your WordPress.com API key is:"*

Studying the Methods of Successful YouTube Personalities and Video Creators

In this final section of the book, we take a look at a few YouTube celebrities who have had success using the site to get their work seen. This represents a first-person account of what it's like to create videos for YouTube and to have your work watched by millions of adoring fans.

Now that you've had a chance to explore both theoretical and practical means for promoting your videos on YouTube, it may be useful to talk to some people who have actually had success on the site. Although there is not one single path to success, it's always useful to compare notes with other YouTube users and creators of online videos. Sometimes, starting at the beginning of the process can reveal the impetus for a successful video, which (on a site like YouTube) can be the combination of several factors, including pure enthusiasm for the creative process itself. The ability of an avid YouTube viewer to pick up on these intangible qualities should not be underestimated.

Becoming a Successful YouTube Personality

Often credited as the first breakout success on YouTube, Brooke Brodack (also known by her user name Brookers) was signed by NBC as the result of her popular YouTube videos, which she directs, edits, and performs herself (see Figure 7-9). When asked about creating videos for the first time, Brooke said, "I always try to avoid forcing videos or ideas out of myself. Never before had I ever written down any of my ideas. I never filmed an idea unless it was *so good* that there was no need for writing it down; it was all in my head: the camera shots I was going to use, the music, everything. I also ad lib mostly all my videos—if there is any speaking, most of it was not planned or written down. I learned to film when I was really young using an analog camera and I had no editing software at the time—it wasn't available like it is today. So when I would film something, it had to be a perfect shot, since we only had one chance to get it right. We would practice, then turn the camera on and film. If we needed a transition, we would put the lens cap on and film blackness. Ah, the good old days."

So how much time does Brooke usually spend on making a video for YouTube? "It depends really; all my videos are different. If I am doing an idea that's forced upon me, that I'm really not

| FIGURE 7-9 | Brooke Brodack represents one of the earliest YouTube personalities to find success. |

too excited about, it could take all day. However, if it's a great idea that I thought of, I get manic and will film until I am practically exhausted because I'm very passionate about the idea. I could get all the filming done in about four hours or less. The editing process, however, could take me an hour or up to two days, depending on how complex the idea is and how much editing is involved. I am a perfectionist!"

It's clear that Brooke is enthusiastic about making videos, and her viewers can see it in videos like "Crazed Numa Fan," "My United States of Whateva," and "Chips," which are prime examples of her unpredictable, kinetic energy. Brooke also acts in her videos, although she says, "I was always fond of being *behind* the camera as opposed to being in front of it, but I didn't really have a choice in the matter. It was a good thing, though, because I have realized how much I truly enjoy acting." Still, there are frustrations that Brooke faces when creating videos, including complex issues like copyright, which YouTube has been cracking down on lately, and this was even more of an issue when she was working for NBC. Brooke uses a lot of music in her videos, and she says, "Music is what inspires me the most. Usually, when I get a good video idea or movie idea, even the *entire* idea was inspired by a song. So having to deal with copyright issues and such, it's really been difficult, and for the longest time it put a damper on the movies I created. I am learning, however, to deal with that, so now I must film, act, edit, and create my own music for my videos. All these things are not really challenges to me because I love what I do, and if I want to make a movie bad enough, I will do it no matter the obstacle, no matter what it takes."

Making Music Videos and Viral Video Hits

Damian Kulash, lead singer and guitarist for the band OK Go is familiar with the challenges of creating music videos, as well as with the recognition that can come from a true viral video hit. When asked about the evolution of the creative process for the song "Here It Goes Again" (which currently has more than 20 million views on YouTube), Damian related the following story, "For years, we had a dance routine that we'd throw into our live show sometimes. It's really pretty shocking and wonderful to see a rock band drop its instruments mid-show and break into choreography; it always sent the shows spinning off into a surreal, euphoric place. Before our second album was released in 2005, we decided we needed a new and improved dance number to go with the new set of songs and asked my sister, Trish Sie, a former professional ballroom dancer, to help us choreograph something to the song "A Million Ways." We taped a rehearsal in my backyard and sent the clip around to a bunch of friends, not thinking of it as a video, per se; it was just the sort of amusing thing your friends might want to see. Within a couple of weeks, the clip was posted on www.ifilm.com, and it started getting passed around. We were pretty amazed when it hit 100,000 views and then 500,000. My friends started getting it from people who didn't know that they were my friends. People's mothers started forwarding it to them."

Damian continued, "This is all before YouTube, of course; at this point, people were just passing around a link to our site or to iFilm or to the video file itself. We started to realize that this clip was doing, in a weird way, exactly what traditional music videos are supposed to. It's not expensive and polished and full of machine-gun edits and Batman camera angles, but it gives people something fun to watch while they're listening to the song, and it puts the band out in front of a whole bunch of new fans. Best of all, people get something we made ourselves. It's actually us and not the artificial promotional image that we're so used to being presented with.

"So we'd stumbled across a new platform, and we decided we should make a clip that was actually intended for it. I called my sister, and we brainstormed for a few hours on how we could keep the spirit of the first clip and its essential simplicity, but ratchet up the intensity of the routine. That's where the treadmill idea came in. By the time we'd made the video, YouTube was just starting out, and we decided to try posting it there.

"To the question of whether or not this video is representative of OK Go's normal creative process…yes. The thrill of making things is why we wound up in a band in the first place. We love chasing down an idea, piecing a project together, making things ourselves, and working with our friends. Having said that, we've also made high-budget videos with famous directors and major-label backing, too. That's a pretty different type of production, and exciting in its own way…but just a different thing."

The response to their video has been incredible. When asked how things have changed for the band since the video for "Here It Goes Again" become popular, Damian responded "It's been pretty amazing to see the effects of the video. It's broken into pop culture in ways that rock bands, and rock videos, usually don't. We've been invited to play in every corner of the world, and found ourselves playing to huge crowds in places like Korea and Taiwan, places where our record wasn't even released prior to the video's success. It's incredible to witness, in such a specific way, the reach of the Internet, and the transformation of pop culture distribution from a top-down model to a bottom-up one. A major label's most strenuous efforts to force-feed us to the masses could never have exposed us to as many fans as our homemade clip has. We're suddenly a household name across the globe. Of course, it's a very weird, and probably temporary, household name. I mean, of the tens of millions of people who've watched our video online, only a fraction are rock and roll fans, people who might go out and pick up our album or come to our show. To most of the world's citizens, we're 'those guys who did the treadmill thing,' and that's all they'll ever know about us. But we're not particularly bothered by that; it's a pretty cool thing to be known for, and we're not interested in fame for the sake of fame. What we want is the opportunity to keep making the things we want to make, and we've certainly got a bigger audience to share them with now than we did before."

Having experienced great success for his band, in part through a site like YouTube, does Damian see YouTube as a good place for artists in general to promote their work? According to Damian, "YouTube is certainly a good place for artists to promote their work. But really, it represents a change in the way things move through culture. I think the idea of 'promoting' work is changing a lot. Most people over the age of 20 are used to an essentially top-down, centralized distribution model in which a few people, or a few corporations, decided what voices to put in front of the limited megaphones, and that's what we all heard.

So we're all accustomed to the idea of 'promoting' work, which is more or less getting the work in front of the megaphone. The newer model of distribution is really more about sharing, about the millions of little choices that millions of real people make—there aren't any central megaphones to get in front of. So I see YouTube less as a "promotional" tool and more as a space, a database, a medium. It's a great new space to exist in and to explore—there's a pretty vertiginous freedom to it—but as an artist, it feels more like an expressive space than a promotional one. For artists in general, the lawless hugeness of YouTube is a real advantage. People anywhere in the world can find your work without the complicated and restrictive system that used to be in the way. For musicians in particular, the clear disadvantage is that it's primarily visual. Our video isn't popular because of the song, it's popular because of the treadmill routine. Most musicians probably don't want to think of the songs they write as being, first and foremost, the soundtrack to the videos they make."

So when Damian isn't making videos, what is he watching on YouTube? "I usually go to YouTube with a reason, trying to find a particular performance that I've heard about or looking at some specific video a friend has sent along. I find, though, that I usually get sucked in and tool around for a little while, getting into some particular niche. I've spent hours on each of these topics at different times: covers of Elvis Costello's "Radio, Radio," baby bears, French people who jump off buildings, Bollywood dancing, freehand drawing competitions, kids with amusing speech impediments, and fundamentalist Christians giving weird home video lectures. I guess I just like discovering nodes of activity. I like stumbling across some topic or theme that a whole bunch of people are interested in and then learning something about it, or at least witnessing their interest. It's sort of like trying to find the genre types for the new medium. Record stores had rock, soul, classical, and jazz. YouTube has extreme sports, child bloopers, virtuoso instrumentalists, and badly recorded political screeds—and about a million others."

Creating a Successful Video Series for YouTube

Any successful video series for YouTube, particularly those produced by low-budget (or no-budget) independent filmmakers, requires a healthy dose of creativity, as well as ingenuity to make the most out of a situation. When asked about the creative process, including how to come up with script and story ideas for YouTube, Francis Stokes (creator of *God, Inc.*, a video series on YouTube that is modeled after the popular sitcom *The Office*) says, "I was really intrigued by the challenge of cramming as much content—humor, pathos, character development, etc.—into just a few minutes of time. It was tough, but I think it improved my writing. In the end, you should always be striving for that kind of quality."

Filming for the series was done in a surprisingly short amount of time. According to Francis, he "filmed the first six episodes of *God, Inc.* in two weekends. It was such a huge cast, and it was a difficult location to get, so I had to just blow through it. No crew—just me and a camera, and my producer, who also played the security guard. If we do any future episodes, we'll see— hopefully we'll have a budget—but the first six were produced for about 80 dollars total!"

As far as the difference between YouTube and other outlets for video creators, Francis doesn't "really see the Web as being that different from any other medium. There are certain factors you have to take into account, like the image quality limitations and the fact that if you bore people they can very easily click away, but there are always factors to consider in any medium. What I love is that a few years ago, there was really no decent way to exhibit short films. If you did a short, there was very little chance anyone would see it, and almost zero chance you'd make any money on it. But now there's a platform for screening them and getting big, potentially huge, audiences, people all over the world. That's thrilling."

When asked whether there were limitations to using YouTube as a tool for promoting video and film work, Francis says that "if I'm speaking to indie filmmakers and videographers who are trying to make their mark or get seen, then no, I feel like the sky's the limit. They're just starting to experiment with ways to monetize videos, both through revenue-share programs and sponsorships and paid advertisements, and there's always the chance to be discovered. There's a whole frontier to be discovered. There is a community on YouTube, people who share videos and support each other and help videos go "viral." Anyone who spends time on it can get in—that's the beauty of the Internet. It's not like Hollywood at all—it's completely democratic. The biggest names on YouTube, both content creators and staff people, have e-mail addresses you can contact and profiles you can comment on. So, you just have to get their attention."

What is Francis up to these days? "I'm working on a few new Web series for YouTube and other video shorts. Meanwhile, I'm developing a TV series for the Sci-Fi Channel, who contacted me after they saw *God, Inc.* And we're in negotiations right now for a TV deal for *God, Inc.* So this success on YouTube has really helped launch my screenwriting and film directing career."

Another YouTube success story is the series *Chad Vader*, created by Aaron Yonda and Matt Sloan, which was also recognized by director George Lucas and featured in many stories about YouTube's potential as a platform for up-and-coming filmmakers (see Figure 7-10). When asked about how they got their start, Matt said, "We actually started making videos on our own for our personal Web site, local screening venues, and the LA-based Channel101.com. After we made *Chad Vader*, we found out that someone else had posted it on YouTube in a kind of crappy, low-res version. So we figured we would post the video on our YouTube channel so people would know who made it. Then it got featured on the front page, and things sort of took off from there."

As far as making the videos, Matt says, "An episode of *Chad Vader* usually takes about a month from start to finish, and typically involves four writers, a cast of eight to twelve people, and a crew of about six to eight. Our other projects tend to be more 'quick and dirty,' utilizing a smaller crew, shorter turnaround time, and looser script."

According to Aaron, "Editing, special effects, and music usually take a week or two. Ultimately, there are about 25 to 30 people involved when you count cast, crew, extras, and postproduction people. And in the first season of *Chad Vader* all these people worked for free, which is one of the main things that made *Chad Vader* possible, since our budget options were limited and we funded it all ourselves."

Clearly, there is an element of luck involved with many YouTube success stories. Getting your videos featured on the Web site can increase your visibility a great deal. However, the creativity of the work (especially considering the limited resources) is undeniable and is the main reason why viewers keep coming back. Of course, humor doesn't hurt (see the pattern?). But where do they come up with the ideas for their videos? According to Matt, "We just kind of come

FIGURE 7-10 *Chad Vader*, created by Aaron Yonda and Matt Sloan, has been quite successful on YouTube.

up with ideas that we both think are funny and then develop them and shoot them. *Chad Vader* is the most scripted thing that we do—we usually end up doing several drafts before we come up with a final script, and that often goes through changes in the shooting and editing process. We like to do a lot of improv and loosely scripted ideas, and that tends to come out in our other projects (Super Shooter, Fun Rangers, McCourt's in Session, etc.)."

Speaking about how their creative process has changed over time, Aaron says, "One thing that has changed, or at least influenced our creative process since we started posting on YouTube, is our close connection with fans of our work. We get a lot of comments on our videos, and although we mainly try to do what we find funny, we also find it interesting to know what the reactions to our videos are. It can be helpful, finding what works and what doesn't work, especially with comedy. And it's cool to have a somewhat closer relationship with our fans."

When asked whether they had any advice for other YouTube video creators, Aaron responded, "Make a lot of videos. Just keep making them and making them, and you'll improve, and eventually, if you stick with it, you'll get some attention. Matt and I have made at least one short video a month since 2002 (one short video with a plot and characters, not a sit-in-front of-the-webcam talky style video, which are easier to shoot). This honed our skills and built our audience until we finally made something that stuck in the form of *Chad Vader*." Matt added, "Just keep doing what you love, rather than what you think people will want to see or what will 'go viral.' If you try to do that, you'll inevitably fail and probably won't have any fun. If you make what you think is funny or interesting or profound or whatever and stick to your instincts, your audience will find you, and even if they don't, you'll still be doing what motivates you and makes you happy, and there's definitely a sense of fulfillment in that."

Glossary

A

Accounts   YouTube provides free accounts to all users, which contain important site features, such as the ability to upload and share your own videos (you do not have to have an account to watch videos on YouTube, however). There are a variety of YouTube account types to choose from, including YouTuber, Comedian, Director, Guru, and Musician. The account type you choose will determine whether users can find your particular channel or videos under that specific category when doing general searches.

Active Sharing   A special feature that allows you to see the names of users who are currently watching a particular video. This feature must be enabled by a user before his or her name will appear on the site.

Address Book   A list of friends and other contacts that is accessible through a member's account. By using the list of contacts in your address book, you can easily send e-mails or share other information with people that you know.

AudioSwap   A special feature that allows you to exchange the existing audio from your video with music that is officially licensed by YouTube.

B

Blog   Web pages that act as a log, or chronicle, of someone's interests, including personal information, news items, or other areas of interest to a particular group of people. Blogs run the gamut from highly personal (what someone ate for breakfast, for example) to commercial and professional sites, such as YouTube's official blog, which can be found at http://youtube.com/blog.

Bulletin   A message that is posted by a user to his or her channel.

C

Category   Videos are organized according to a preselected category, as defined by the user who uploaded the video. Categories in YouTube include Comedy, Entertainment, Film & Animation, Music, Pets & Animals, and many more. YouTube includes a Categories tab to easily access videos by this set of criteria.

Channel   A member's page on YouTube, where they can upload videos, post their user profile, post bulletins, and more. Users can visit a particular channel directly or by browsing channels using the Channels tab.

Comments   Text responses left by viewers of another user's video or channel.

Contest   Users can compete in a variety of contests by submitting their own videos. Contests can be accessed through the Community tab on the YouTube Web site.

D

Developer API   The application programming interface (API) used by programmers and Web developers who want access to key components of the YouTube video library and community features. Visit the Developer area of the YouTube Web site at http://youtube.com/dev for further information.

E

Embedding   The ability to place YouTube videos on other Web pages or blogs using code that is generated for each video already uploaded to YouTube. The embed code for each video appears to the right of the video on its Watch page.

F

Favorite   A Video that you like and choose to save to a list that is associated with your account. Favorites are saved for later viewing or browsing by visitors to your channel page.

Featured Videos   Videos that are selected by the editors of YouTube and that most often appear on the YouTube home page, individual category pages, channel pages, and other areas of the YouTube Web site.

Flash   A cross-platform plug-in for Web browsers (available from Adobe) that enables users to watch YouTube videos and other special content online. Flash is currently the most common plug-in for Web browsers, which makes it an ideal format for supporting the widest range of users.

FLV   Flash Video format (FLV), which is used by YouTube to play videos on its Web site and other places where its videos are embedded. When you upload any video to YouTube, it is converted by the site into the FLV format, which makes it accessible to the widest range of users. Apart from accessibility, other benefits of the FLV format include the ability to easily scale video and add interactive layers, which enables the special features that can be seen in an embedded video player.

Friends   People who you can invite to participate in private discussions, share confidential videos with, and include in other special activities involved with your channel.

G

Groups   Allow users to share videos with each other and have discussions based on a particular topic or theme. Users can find available groups listed under the Community tab.

H

H.264   An advanced video codec (compression and decompression method) based on the MPEG-4 standard, which is currently being used for a variety of purposes, including the encoding of YouTube videos for devices like Apple's iPhone and AppleTV.

History   A list of the recent videos you have watched on YouTube, which is accessible through a History link at the top of most YouTube Web pages.

Honors   Statistics that are kept for YouTube videos with the best ratings (such as videos that were viewed the most this week).

M

Metadata   Essentially, data about your data, or information that is used to describe your videos, including their titles, descriptions, tags, and more. You can add this information when you upload a video or edit it later through your account.

P

Playlist   A list of videos that you create by adding your favorite videos to them or by organizing videos that you uploaded. Playlists allow you to better share selections of videos with other users, including visitors to your channel page.

Q

Quick Capture   A special feature that allows you to post a video directly to YouTube using your webcam.

QuickList   A list of videos that is saved for quick, convenient viewing during an online session. It can be created by simply clicking the plus sign (+) symbol that appears on each video's thumbnail image while browsing.

R

Rating   The number of stars that is applied to a video based on an assessment of its quality by other users, with a maximum rating of five stars.

Related Videos   Videos that are determined by YouTube to be relevant in some way to the video that you are currently watching.

Remixer   A new tool (designed by Adobe) that allows you to edit videos directly on the YouTube Web site using videos that you have already uploaded to your channel.

RSS   Really Simple Syndication (RSS) is a subscription process that can be added to any Web page, which makes it possible for subscribers to receive automatic updates of new content, or feeds, that are added to that site. RSS feeds can be viewed using a qualifying Web browser or special software that functions as an RSS reader.

S

Share Videos   Links to a YouTube video that are sent to someone by e-mail.

Streams   Real-time chats where videos can be watched and commented on by viewers at the same time.

Subscription   Members can choose to subscribe to another user's channel, which allows them to get automatic updates when new videos and bulletins have been added by that user.

T

Tags   Keywords that are associated with a particular video and that make the video easier to locate during searches or other associative processes on YouTube. Tags are added when a user uploads a video to YouTube.

TestTube   An area of the YouTube Web site where new site features are made available for preview and testing purposes prior to an official launch.

V

Video Response   The video equivalent of a text comment, where users can upload a video of their own that they think adds to the discussion of a particular video.

Viral Video   A video whose popularity spreads through being shared by people on the Internet, often through e-mail, social networking sites (including YouTube), and posting on blogs.

Vlog   A term that refers to a video blog, or the video equivalent of a traditional blog, which is most often used to present video diaries and monologues to the camera, although it may also include a general collection of relevant or newsworthy video entries.

W

Watch Page   YouTube uses this term to refer to the page where a full-sized video plays (along with all of the other information for the video, such as its description, comments, etc.).

Index